Language and Teaching

A PSYCHOLOGICAL VIEW

Peter Herriot

METHUEN & CO LTD

11 NEW FETTER LANE LONDON EC4

First published in 1971
© 1971 by Peter Herriot
Printed in Great Britain by
Cox & Wyman Ltd.
Fakenham, Norfolk

SBN 416 65200 X (hardback)
SBN 416 65210 7 (paperback)

Distributed in the U.S.A.
by Barnes & Noble Inc.

Language and Teaching
a psychological view

Contents

1 Communication   page 1

  1 Communication as a process   1

  2 Communication and teaching   5

  3 Factors affecting the success of communication   6

2 Some Definitions   10

  1 The psychologist   10

  2 Language   13

  3 Thinking   14

  4 Language and thinking   15

3 Language Behaviour as a Skill   18

  1 The nature of skill   18

  2 Phonological skill   20

  3 Grammatical skill   22

  4 Semantic skill   24

  5 Non-linguistic skill   26

  6 Linguistic skill   27

4 Language Acquisition   30

  1 Productivity   30

  2 Phonological skill   30

  3 Grammatical skill   32

  4 Semantic skill   34

  5 An overview   37

  6 Implications   39

✓ *5 Language Deficit and Remediation*   41

   1 Environmental deprivation – its nature   41

   2 Environmental deprivation – its causes   43

   3 Strategies of remediation   44

   4 Tactics of remediation   46

   5 Specific language deficit   50

6 Language and Thinking   52

   1 Language and thinking   52

   2 Internalization   53

   3 Implications of internalization   54

   4 The development of thinking: operational thinking   55

   5 The development of thinking: concrete and formal
      operations   57

   6 The teacher's use of language to assist development
      of thinking   59

   7 Summary   61

7 Language and Personal Development   62

   1 Nature of the self-concept   62

   2 Development of the self-concept   63

   3 The self-concept in adolescence   64

   4 The development of attitudes and morality   66

   5 Language and the early development of the self-concept
      and attitudes   68

   6 Language and the systematization of the self-concept and
      attitudes   70

8 *Language and Social Development*   73

  1 The development of social roles   73

  2 The developed skills of role-playing   74

  3 Language and the development of social roles   76

  4 Language and the developed skills of role-playing   77

  5 Implications for teaching   79

  6 Summary   80

9 *Language Behaviour in the Classroom*   82

  1 Communication   82

  2 Regulation   84

  3 Language and skilled reading   86

  4 Language and learning to read   88

  5 Language and writing   92

  6 Summary   94

10 *Psychological Background*   95

  1 Psychological theory   95

  2 Some further reading   97

Bibliography   101

Glossary   105

Index   108

Foreword

This book is intended primarily as a text for students training to be teachers, and for any others whose knowledge of psychology is not considerable. The aim of the book is to describe the psychological functions of language; language is used to communicate and to regulate behaviour. The development of these functions, their connection with cognitive, personal, and social development, and their implications for the classroom are discussed.

The author has written this book to be read through quickly. It outlines an overall point of view which is presented in as logical a sequence as possible. It is not intended so much as a repository of information as a stimulus of ideas. These ideas will, it is hoped, concern the aims and methods of teaching rather than theoretical disagreements in psychology. For the part played by language in education has for long been overlooked by psychologists and undue prominence given to oversimple models of learning.

I would like to thank my friends and colleagues Margaret Bates, John Butcher, Dorothy Jeffree, and Geoffrey Roberts for their helpful comments on the manuscripts; and Judith Wilding for typing the entire book and writing the index. All errors and obscurities that remain are my own.

1 Communication

Consider a lecture and a conversation. Suppose that the lecture is of a formal nature, with the lecturer either reading from notes or sticking to them very closely; and suppose that the conversation is between husband and wife deciding where they should go for an evening's entertainment. What features have these two situations in common, and in what ways do they differ?

Firstly they are both examples of *communication*. For in both cases people are behaving in such a way that they are affecting the behaviour of others; and they are doing so in a symbolic and indirect rather than in a direct way. Both these criteria seem necessary for communication to occur; I may kick someone downstairs, thereby affecting his behaviour, but in a very direct way. If, however, I were to call him downstairs, or merely ring the dinner gong, communication has taken place. For I have used the utterance or the gong as cues, or signals, to affect his behaviour. To return to our two situations: the lecturer, too, is seeking to affect the behaviour of his audience. Hopefully, he is trying to enable them to analyse a topic in a more useful way; possibly he is aiming at producing certain specific responses in a written examination. The husband and wife, too, are aiming at affecting their behaviour by communicating, in this case at going somewhere together.

These two situations are not so much events as *processes*. That is, there is no sudden transition from when communication has not occurred to when it has. Rather, there is a very complex series of events, each of which affects the others. In the case of the lecture, the lecturer has to give utterance in an audible and comprehensible way, and the audience has to perceive, or identify, what he is saying and understand it. This series of events requires some very complex skills indeed. The lecturer has to select and relate his subject matter, choose the words to express himself by, order those words grammatically in sentences, and articulate them clearly. The audience has to identify

2 Language and Teaching

what he is saying, using the sounds he makes and their surrounding context to do so; and they have to relate their perception of the utterance to what they know about the subject under discussion. These skills will be described in more detail in Chapter 3. Obviously, in the communication situation, many of them are occurring simultaneously.

There are, however, differences between our two communication situations. The first difference is the amount of *feedback* which occurs in each of them. The function of feedback is to allow a system to regulate itself. For example, a thermostatically controlled radiator is just such a self-regulating system. The radiator emits heat into the room until the room temperature reaches such a point that the thermostat switches it off; when the room cools again, the thermostat switches the radiator on. The result is a stable and steady system. Putting it another way, the radiator uses information from its environment in order to modify its behaviour. Now take the case of the lecturer; he is emitting utterances just as the radiator is emitting heat. But there is little feedback information to make him modify what he is doing. He may notice that the audience is scribbling furiously and slow down a bit as a result; or he may see that they are dozing off, or chatting to each other, so he raises his voice. He may even perceive a look of puzzlement or boredom on some faces, in which case he will ask 'That's clear enough, isn't it?' (a rhetorical question) or try to crack a joke. But the point is that he will not change the basic nature of his utterances. There will, in other words, be little feedback; as a result, there is unlikely to be a steady state, with the lecturer producing utterances capable of being understood by the audience. Instead, he will guess, probably incorrectly, the level at which he should pitch his lecture. It is worth noting at this point that this book is an excellent example of absence of feedback.

Consider, by way of contrast, the conversation. The husband may start off by suggesting an evening at the pub, to which his wife might reply, 'Well . . .', in a certain tone of voice. Or she might even say no! As a result the husband modifies his behaviour, suggesting instead a visit to the theatre (where at least there's a bar). At this his wife perks up. She may say that that's a good idea, but wouldn't it be nicer to go to the pictures. Her behaviour too, has been modified by outside events; for she has heard her husband change his original proposal for another closer to her own preference, the cinema. She therefore suggests this preferred activity, thinking it has a good chance of acceptance. However, she had not realized that the reason her husband suggested the theatre was that there was a bar there. Therefore his subsequent short-tempered refusal to even consider the cinema is her cue to suggest a licensed restaurant. In this situation, feedback is constantly operating. Moreover, it is operating in a far more complex way than in the case of the lecture. For here, the husband is modifying his behaviour as a result of its effects on his wife, and the wife is modifying her behaviour as a result of its effects on her husband. In other words the wife's utterances (for example) are acting both as behaviour that is being modified and also as cues to the husband to modify his behaviour.

A final difference between the two situations, the lecture and the conversation, is the part which *language* plays in communication. The lecturer's audience has to concentrate carefully on what he is saying, since there are few other cues available. He is probably too far away from them for his facial expression to be clearly visible, and few lecturers gesture in the grand manner. If he is reading, he is unlikely to break off and use the blackboard. Because he is so dependent on language to communicate, the lecturer will probably employ it in the optimal way. He will structure his sentences to provide maximum *redundancy*. In other words, he will include many words that would not be strictly necessary if he were presenting his subject in the briefest way possible. He will include a lot of 'howevers', 'therefores', 'in point of facts'; he will ask himself questions which he will then proceed to answer; and he will define his terms. All these procedures involve using extra language, which, hopefully, decrease the uncertainty of the audience as to what he is talking about. (Compare the account of being burgled you would give to a friend over the telephone with the telegram you would send.) There is, of course, one possible drawback in the use of redundancy; the lecturer may use so many 'therefores' and 'howevers', he may define his terms so thoroughly, that it becomes impossible to remember at the end of a sentence what he said at the beginning!

Contrast the conversation. The husband and wife are employing many cues besides the language they use to each other. They are face to face, and so the facial cues are available. In the account of their conversation I gave earlier, I said that the wife perked up when her husband suggested the theatre. Perking up is signalled by all sorts of events. Perhaps she smiled a little, and replied more quickly to that suggestion than to the previous one. The part played by the eyes in face-to-face communication is particularly important. In this case they could signal interest in the proposal by making contact with the husband's eyes. Eye-contact is often used to signal when one is going to stop speaking or when one wishes the other person to stop speaking. If you place two equally talkative people, a man and a woman, opposite each other, they will probably talk equal lengths of time. However, if you put a board between them so that eye-contact is impossible, the man monopolizes the conversation. He is less sensitive to eye-contact and its implications than the woman. Furthermore, there are subtle aspects of speaking which are probably open to face-to-face conversers but not to the lecturer. When the husband proposed the pub, his wife probably paused slightly before replying, then said 'well' in such a way as to lengthen the vowel and raise the pitch at the end of the word; try it. In addition, of course, the husband and wife have their expectations of how the other will behave, based on their experience of each other. In our example, the wife probably expected her husband to want a drink, although it required several exchanges before this expectation modified her behaviour and she suggested a licensed restaurant. Such similar expectations cannot be assumed in the lecture, where the lecturer may not know to what extent his audience is familiar with the subject.

2 COMMUNICATION AND TEACHING

The view of communication which we have been considering differs considerably from the way many people talk about teaching. I have stressed both the production of the message *and* its comprehension. Above all, I have emphasized the importance of feedback. The producer of the message cannot know whether he has been understood or not unless the receiver gives some evidence that he has understood. This evidence will act as feedback in the following way. If the receiver indicates by his behaviour that he has understood, then the producer can continue with the message; if there is any doubt, the producer can repeat or rephrase the message. Clearly, for such feedback to occur, the receiver must behave in some visible or audible way. In our everyday conversations we get this sort of feedback; if we ask someone to fetch a pin, and he arrives carrying a bin, we know he has misperceived; or if we ask him to give us a ring and he sends us a piece of jewellery, we know he has misunderstood (perhaps). In both cases we can change and expand the message to ensure correct perception and understanding.

In the case of *teaching*, there must, similarly, be evidence of understanding. Otherwise the teacher cannot adapt his instruction to the needs of the child. It is fortunate that the current emphasis is on learning by active behaviour. There are many psychological grounds for supporting this emphasis. But from the point of view of communication, the importance of activity is that it provides *evidence* of understanding. Many programmes employed in programmed instruction employ feedback in a similar way; if the learner makes the desired response he goes on to the next step; if he makes a mistake, he goes back to a previous step, depending on the nature of his mistake. It is precisely the same with active methods of learning: the teacher should be able to tell from the child's behaviour as he tries to solve some problem whether he understands the principles involved or not. Of course, this means that activity methods must be very carefully planned so that the teacher can infer with confidence from the child's behaviour whether or not he does understand.

The need to adapt instruction to accord with feedback is ignored by those teachers who speak of 'giving them the stuff'. What is implied by this rather ugly metaphor is a passive feeding process of pre-digested material. Great emphasis is laid on the production side of the communication process but little attention given to the reception side. The 'stuff' may be very carefully pre-digested; it may be arranged in extremely neat and tidy packages. But the assumption is that the receiver structures the message in the same way as the producer. All that we know about children argues against this; they actively structure what they see and hear, rather than passively receive it. And the way they structure depends on the stage of development they have reached in their language and their thinking. For example, the five- to six-year-old is likely to be affected by the most noticeable feature of the situation. He will say that there are more items in a longer row than in a shorter row of objects, even though the shorter row in fact contains more. Children, in other words, will structure incoming information in a different way from an adult. Of course, the teacher may be skilled enough to pre-package the material in the same way as the child structures it. Even so, children need to actively impose a structure rather than passively receive it; so if too much structure, even of the appropriate kind, is presented, the aim of the process is frustrated.

In brief, then, communication in teaching, as any other situation, is a process. It involves activity in producing messages, whether verbal or non-verbal, by the teacher; it involves activity in perceiving and understanding those messages, by the children; and, most important, it involves activity by the teacher in understanding the children's activity and adapting her own to accord with the feedback the children provide.

3 FACTORS AFFECTING THE SUCCESS OF COMMUNICATION

Successful communication, then, occurs when children understand the messages the teacher produces. What factors determine whether communication is going to be successful or not? The amount of feedback obtained is one such factor within the situation itself. But there are many other factors, some of them external to the situation. They will be outlined now, and described in more detail later in the book.

Firstly, there are *the communicants* themselves. We have already noted that the tasks of producing and understanding messages demand extremely complex skills. They demand both specifically linguistic skills and often, general cognitive (thinking) skills. The obvious difficulty in teaching is that the producer and the receiver are usually at different stages of development in these skills. We shall see from Chapter 6 (thinking) and to a lesser extent from Chapter 4 (language) that these differences are not merely differences of degree but differences of kind; that is, adults are not merely *more* skilful than children, but they have *different ways* of doing things. These differences are not only due to the different levels of development reached by children and teachers; they are also due to cultural background. Most teachers are middle-class and most children workingclass (leaving these terms undefined for the moment), and this too, has important effects on communication (see Chapter 5).

The second factor which affects efficiency of communication is its context. There is often a fairly well-defined *social context* for communication. For example, the lecturer soon shows that he is not asking questions to find out, but rather stating his own position on the subject. The social context of that particular communication thus prevents meaningful feedback from the audience. On the other hand modern marriage in Western societies is an institution which often involves joint decisionmaking, so the social context of our other example encourages feedback. In the classroom (see Chapter 9), the social context depends largely on the teacher and the role she assumes (see Chapter 8); on the nature and size of the groups of her pupils; and on their age. This latter point is worth expanding; in a class of adolescents, the social contexts of communication may be in conflict. The adolescent, in communicating with the teacher, may break the communication rules of his group of friends. The discussion of a poem is the sort of situation which might give rise to this conflict.

B

There is also an *environmental context to* communication. Very often, language is used to refer to features of the environment. We point at objects or events and say things about them. This is particularly true of instruction, where the teacher frequently makes *reference*. It is worth noting that you can not only make statements about things you refer to – 'That's a kettle, and you boil water in it'; you can also ask questions – 'That's a kettle. What do you use it for?' In order for a reference to be understood, the speaker must refer unambiguously to the item referred to (the referent). For example, if the kettle is right next to a saucepan on the shelf, the speaker might have to say 'The one with the spout is the kettle', or 'The bigger one is the kettle'. In other words, the more possible alternative referents, the more the reader has verbally to distinguish between them. This possibility of confusion is extremely important in education. When visual aids are used, or actual material, accidental properties of the items must not interfere with the feature being referred to. If a child is being taught number, then the accidental fact that some of the items are red and others green should not obscure the essential feature of number. This caution is particularly necessary in the case of subnormal children, who find it especially difficult to 'screen out' irrelevant features of the situation. Is the profusion of pictures and objects in the modern infant and primary classroom always desirable?

A final factor affecting the success of communication is the nature of the *change* in the receiver which it causes. If we suppose that children have ways of structuring what they see and hear, then the message must be of such a kind that they can apply their structures to it. This is known as *assimilating* what one sees and hears to one's own modes of language and thinking. However, one of the teacher's aims is to assist the development of the child's modes of language and of thinking. He will therefore present messages which make the child change these modes to accord with the evidence. This is known as *accommodating* them to deal with the discrepancy between what the child expects and what the evidence actually shows.

An example: one expects water to fall out of a beaker turned upside-down; but this expectation is not fulfilled when cardboard is placed over the beaker when it is upright, and then turned over. As a result, the ways of thinking to which one had assimilated the situation had to be accommodated to account for the discrepant evidence. Perhaps the most important point to note is that accommodation does not seem to occur, for children in particular, if the new evidence is excessively divergent from the expectations based on existing modes of language or thinking. (Most of a sect who believed that the end of the world would occur on a certain day were unwilling to change their beliefs when prophecy failed.) This is why it is necessary to gear communication to the development level of the child; for if the message is markedly in advance of his own modes of language or thinking, no accommodation will occur. This is a particular danger when language alone is the means of communication. The connection between language and thinking is very complex (see Chapters 2 and 5); clearly, however, it is very easy to use language which is apparently understood as language, but to which the child's ways of thinking do not match up.

In summary, it is evident that communication is a situation in which all sorts of factors are important. For communication is between people, and therefore the skills those people employ, the way they think, the relations between them, and the environment in which communication occurs, are all vital. However, the emphasis in the remainder of this book will be on language; for firstly language is the distinctly human mode of communication; and secondly, its relation with thinking and therefore with education is of primary importance.

2 Some Definitions

This is going to be a rather piecemeal chapter. It starts by saying what psychologists do and what use they think they are. It continues by looking from a psychologist's point of view at the words language and thinking. And it concludes by giving some reasons why language and thinking and their relation to each other are important for teachers. Such a chapter is necessary because we plunged straight away in the previous chapter into an analysis of communication. It seemed reasonable to do this, however, for communication is the process teachers are actually involved in; and to communicate is one of the two main functions of language.

Many readers, particularly physical scientists, will already have concluded that all social scientists employ woolly and ill-defined terms because they are trying to deal in a so-called scientific way with matters which are not amenable to scientific analysis. And they will not have excluded the present writer from their criticisms. So allow me to define some of the terms which were used so freely in the previous chapter.

In the course of definition, it may become clear that psychologists have certain characteristic ways of looking at things. In case it doesn't become clear, I will outline them now! First, and most important, the psychologist analyses a situation in terms of what it is and why it is; he is not concerned with what it ought to be. Second, he concerns himself with human behaviour, the regulation of that behaviour by the brain, and the external events which give the signal for the behaviour to occur. Third, he is ready to apply his knowledge of human behaviour to a worthwhile objective, providing it is made clear to him what that objective is.

But he faces very considerable difficulties in these aims. Firstly, human behaviour is a subject from which it is almost impossible to exclude value judgements. So the psychologist has to be continuously on his guard not to introduce his own values into his descriptions and explanations. This is particularly true when he uses technically words which in ordinary language have strong connotative overtones. For example, to describe a person as of above average intelligence should be purely descriptive for the psychologist, but it is often treated as praise if used by the layman; for high intelligence is considered a desirable attribute by our own and most other societies.

Even more difficult is the application of any knowledge the psychologist has about human behaviour to a practical objective. For the knowledge is derived from controlled experiments, while the application is to uncontrolled situations. *Control* in a scientific experiment means that all other variables in the experiment are kept constant and only the variable(s) in which the experimenter is interested is manipulated. For example, the experimenter might hypothesize that normal adults can solve a reasoning problem if they are given a verbal clue more easily than if they are given a visual clue. To answer this question, the only variable which must change is the nature of the clue. Everything else must be held constant – the problem must be presented in the same way to the subjects of the experiment; the subjects themselves (who will be divided into two groups, each receiving one type of clue), must be equated for intelligence; the experimenter in charge of the proceedings should probably be the same for all subjects; the same maximum time should be given for solution.

The reason for all these precautions is this: if the problem is solved more quickly and efficiently by the group who received the verbal clue, one wishes to say that their superiority is due to the verbal clue being more helpful than the visual one. But if this group is more intelligent on average than the other group, then their superiority at solving the problem could be due to their intelligence, not to the nature of the clue. This is the sort of controlled evidence on which psychologists base their statements about human behaviour.

But psychology is not an advanced science; there are a great many variables which might affect human behaviour, and few of them have been investigated experimentally. Of those which have, not all are theoretically important. So the psychologist cannot speak with confidence in many areas, and his knowledge is limited. The greatest difficulty comes when he is asked to apply what knowledge he has to a practical situation.

Practical situations (such as teaching) are not controlled in the same way as a scientific experiment is controlled. There are many factors operating at the same time. The teacher might give a verbal clue to one child and a visual clue to another, but the children may be of different intelligence and social class; one may be further on with the problem than the other; they may be using different materials; one child may be on his own while the other is in a group; and so on. In this case, all that the psychologist can do is try to pick out what he thinks are the crucial variables in the situation (for example, intelligence, social class, and whether the child is working on his own or not). He will pick these out because of his knowledge of experiments which show that each of these variables can be important in problem solving.

However, he is faced with a situation in which he does not know to what extent each variable is present. And most important of all, he doesn't know how these variables *interact*; for example, it might be true that middle-class children might find verbal clues more helpful than visual, but that working-class children might find visual more helpful than verbal. Or, more complex still, more intelligent children might find verbal clues more helpful than visual when they are on their own, but not when they are in a group; whereas less intelligent children might find verbal more helpful than visual when they are in a group but not when they are on their own (draw graphs to see what these interactions mean). The psychologist can investigate such interactions in more complex experiments, but the point remains that his experiments are controlled whereas the classroom is not.

So, really, the psychologist's comments on teaching are just one sort of informed opinion; experienced or perceptive teachers may well predict far more accurately which sort of clue is going to yield better results in any given situation; above all, the teacher is going to know more about individual children than any outsider, so she can take more variables into account in her prediction. In brief, the psychologist can only emphasize the things he has found important in his experiments; and he can offer a certain detached way of analysing situations.

2 LANGUAGE

Now to define, from a psychological point of view, some of the terms used in the previous chapter. The terms which recur most often are *language* and *thinking*. We will first discard some of the usages of these words in everyday speech, not because they are in any sense wrong, but because they are not useful for psychological analysis.

We speak of bad language, meaning swearing; foreign or native languages; we sometimes say 'They speak their own language' meaning that some group, although they speak English, are incomprehensible as far as we are concerned. More misleadingly, we sometimes speak of language as though it were a set of words with meanings. Two basic fallacies are involved here. The first is to consider language as a *set of items*. The most important thing about language is that it is structured, not a string of isolated items joined together. There are, in other words, general principles behind the way people speak and listen, produce and understand; we do not simply listen to each word, recognize its 'meaning', and 'add up' the meanings. It is these principles which determine the way one understands the newspaper headlines 'dog bites man', 'man bites dog', 'man bitten by dog', 'dog bitten by man'.

The second basic fallacy is to talk at all of words having *meanings*, as though there were one event, a word, and another, the meaning attached to it. What is *the* meaning of 'ring', 'train', 'fan'? You reply that each word has several meanings. What then is the meaning of 'honesty', 'love', 'beauty', 'anger'? You reply that these words do not have meanings in the outside world, but are rather concepts in the mind. What about 'and', 'but', 'although'? I don't know what you reply now! And why do 'man bites dog', and 'dog bites man' differ, since they are the same words? Because of their order? Then why do 'man bites dog' and 'dog bitten by man' mean the same (roughly) although they are in different order? The point is, that words are not separate, individual items, nor are they used just to refer to things or to concepts. Reference may be one of the functions of language, but it is not the only function. Language is used to persuade, to make people laugh, and for many other purposes which do not involve reference. So we must conclude that language is not just a string of words, each with its own 'meaning'.

From a psychological point of view, what is language? A psychologist always starts off with observable behaviour, so the first thing he is interested in is language behaviour, or the utterance of and listening to speech. Speech is not a random series of sounds; on the contrary, it is a highly systematic structure. The sounds of speech, their combination in words, the order of words, and their identity are all different parts of this structure. The psychologist is particularly interested in discovering those processes in the brain which must be supposed to exist in order to account for such complex behaviour. For since it is the brain which regulates behaviour, complex processes must be supposed to underlie complex behaviour. These processes I term *language*.

3 THINKING

The term *thinking* is also used in many ways in everyday speech. We often say a person is thinking when he is daydreaming and doing nothing; when we remember and recall a past event, we are said to be thinking of it; we are told to think what we're doing if our attention wanders; and we are asked what we think about an issue when our opinions are being canvassed. Psychologically, the term thinking is used of the processes in the brain which regulate complex behaviour. For example, solving a problem or painting a picture are very complicated activities, and they demand similarly complex and perhaps novel combinations of processes in the brain.

So we are using *language* as a term to denote the psychological processes which regulate speech (which we call language behaviour). Linguists also use the term language, but they use it of the abstract system which they use to describe speech. There is no need to assume that their system describes what goes on in the brain. And we are using *thinking* as a term to refer to the processes which regulate other forms of complex behaviour.

4 LANGUAGE AND THINKING

Why should teachers be interested in what a psychologist has to say about language and thinking? Perhaps the most important area for teachers is not language, or thinking, but *how language can help thinking.* A great deal of teaching is based on the assumption that it can. The connection between the two will be considered in detail in Chapter 6, but a few general comments can be made here. The first major point is that both are *developmental processes.* The language of children approximates more and more closely to that of adults as the child grows older; so does their thinking, although in this case there are more discernible stages through which thinking passes before it becomes adult in nature. If, therefore, language is to be used to aid thinking, neither the language nor the thinking demanded of the child must grossly exceed the child's developmental level (see p. 52).

If one wishes to improve language, then one will introduce slightly more advanced language but keep the thinking task well within the child's range of thinking; if one wishes to develop thinking, one will use well-established language in slightly novel task situations. For example, suppose one is trying to teach conservation of number to a child who has not yet attained it; that is, one is trying to teach him that five objects are five objects whether for example they are strung out in a long line or are packed close together. One might ask the child, 'How many are there in this row? . . . And how many in this row? Count them.' Now the teacher has uttered these instructions. But if the child is going to regulate his thinking by his own language, he will have to utter the instructions to himself. He will have to tell himself to

and be able to do so. It is therefore vital that the language
our that the teacher uses is within the child's range of
standing. For the child can then use it himself, aloud
ntly, to modify his behaviour in a situation demanding a
more advanced level of thinking. If he cannot understand the
instructions, he will certainly be unlikely to adapt his behaviour
to solve the task.

One error, then, that a teacher can make is to use excessively
advanced *language* to explain a task. Another is to be misled by
the child's mastery of language to try to teach tasks demanding a
level of *thinking* which is way beyond what the child is at
present capable of. Perhaps the latter is a more obvious danger;
some children, particularly middle-class extraverts, are linguistically so facile that the teacher assumes they are capable of
thinking in comparably developed ways. Of course, it is very
difficult to compare level of language development with level of
thinking development; but perhaps linguistic skill is more
noticeable; and perhaps teachers are not always aware of the
sorts of behaviour that are evidence of advanced thinking.

The first reason, then, why teachers should be interested in
language is that it can help thinking. It was clear in our example
of teaching conservation of number (see p. 15) that before the
child could direct his thinking by means of his own language, he
had to understand what the teacher said. So the second reason
for interest in language is that it is the usual medium of *communication*; and that having been understood, it can then be
employed to help thinking. The efficiency of the communication
process (see Chapter 1) is therefore a vital pre-requisite for
teaching. For if communication does not occur, then the child
may not have at his disposal the language or other symbolic
means which the teacher wishes him to use to help his thinking.

There is, therefore, every justification for trying to encourage
the language development of children and engaging in specific
language remediation when there is a deficit. However, it does
not follow that language development is best encouraged by
teaching which concentrates on language behaviour in isolation. Language behaviour is always used for a communicative
purpose; one wishes to refer to something to direct someone's

attention to it, or one asks a question to obtain information, or one makes a request or utters a command in order to get someone to do something. To instruct language skills isolated from their communicative purpose is to risk the possibility that what you teach never transfers from the teaching situation to any other situation. The child may never use the improved grammatical structure nor the wider choice of words you have taught him anywhere other than the 'language lesson'.

The reason, then, for analysing language behaviour in detail in Chapter 3, its acquisition in Chapter 4, and its remediation in Chapter 5 is because *language is a medium for communication and a tool for thinking*. This is a very powerful combination of functions.

You will notice that I have not said that language is necessary for thinking, only that it can help. How otherwise can deaf children communicate and think? And I certainly have not identified language and thinking as being the same thing; I have not said, in other words, that one thinks in words. You may say that you do, but then you may not really think as you think you think.

3 Language Behaviour as a Skill

I THE NATURE OF SKILL

Driving is a skill. The psychologist means by this statement something more than that driving is complex and difficult. He means that the skilled driver makes what is difficult look easy, and he is prepared to suggest some of the tricks the driver uses to do so.

The skilled driver *anticipates*, so he adapts his present direction and speed to accord with the situation as it will be in a few seconds' time. The tennis player anticipates by moving to a position where he can deal with his opponent's next stroke before that stroke is made. Both men do this by using previous evidence to construct what is going to happen.

The skilled driver, secondly, performs many actions *automatically*. A gear change, for example, is an automatic action once he has decided to carry it out. For the learner, a gear change is not a single action, but a sequence of individual actions each of which needs his concentration. So the skilled driver can attend to other things once he has decided to change gear and started to do so. Because the whole sequence of changing gear is automated, he can plan his next operation while performing the present one; automation makes anticipation possible. As a result the transition from changing gear to the next operation, for example, accelerating, is smooth, since he has already thought out what the next operation is. There results that typical smoothness of performance which comes from skill.

Another feature of skill is that it is dependent upon accurate analysis of *feedback*. The driver continuously adjusts the steering in accordance with the visual feedback, which he obtains from his position on the road. He changes gear in accordance with the auditory feedback he receives from the engine. In both cases, there is an optimum state in which he wants to be – a certain position on the road and a certain engine speed.

Related to these features of skill is the possibility of overall *planning* of skilled behaviour. The driver can plan the driving of his car out of his garage and on to the road so as to face in a certain direction. He can plan in advance because he can *anticipate* the effect of his operations. He can also substitute one piece of *automated* behaviour for another; for example, within the overall plan, he can decide to back out looking over his shoulder rather than in the wing mirror.

Language behaviour is skilled behaviour, and follows the same principles as driving. One *plans* overall the general nature of one's utterance when, for example, one decides to ask the time. Within this overall plan, there are different levels of skill, all of which are necessary to the plan. One must select the right words and phrases; one must order them and structure them grammatically; and one must articulate them accurately. Within the plan, it is possible to choose one of several alternatives without destroying the overall plan. One can say 'Excuse me, but could you tell me the time?' or 'Excuse me, can you tell me the time, please?'

Because one plans in advance, one *anticipates* what one is going to say considerably ahead of when one says it. This becomes clear when people make the occasional slip of introducing an element from what they are going to say, for example, 'Excuse me, but could you time me the tell?' It is also evident from the annoying habit of some listeners of telling us what we are going to say next before we actually say it: they finish our sentence for us.

Of course, language behaviour is *automated* into chunks. When a typist is taking dictation, she will wait until at least a phrase has been uttered before she starts writing. This is because she remembers and types in phrases. In our example, the phrase 'excuse me' was automated – its articulation needed no conscious control, the selection of words with which to address a passer-by probably 'came naturally', and the ordering of the words grammatically was automatic, since there was no risk of saying 'me excuse', or 'excuse I'.

And finally, language behaviour requires *feedback*. We need to hear ourselves talking in order to articulate adequately.

This is shown when the sound of one's own utterances is delayed by a loop in a tape recorder for one-fifth of a second, so that one only hears what one is saying after this slight delay. Speech is completely distorted, with vowels elongated and consonants stuttered.

2 PHONOLOGICAL SKILL

Thus language behaviour as a whole exhibits all the features of skill. We will now analyse each of the sub-skills in turn, starting with the lowest level, the *phonological* level. This deals with the perception and articulation of speech sounds. It is first worth asking why we are calling this sub-skill the lowest level of language skill. It is because the choice of words and their ordering leave very little uncertainty indeed as to the identity of a speech sound. In our example, the listener's mistake 'Excuse me, but could cue tell me the time' is unlikely; unlikely because the grammar leads us to expect a pronoun and the sense makes 'cue' an obvious intrusion. We probably plan overall when we select the 'content' words, and the grammar and the articulation fall into place as we go along. This is not so true of the listener as of the speaker. The listener has to guess what the speaker's overall plan of the sentence is, using the beginning of the sentence as his clues. Of course, he may guess what the speaker is going to say from the non-linguistic context of the utterance. The way we use the sense and the grammar of the sentence to guess the identity of the sound becomes evident when we listen to a telephone message over interference; or when we hear a Chinese speaker say 'Velly nice flied lice'.

This last example leads us to the question of how the phonological sub-skill works. The Chinese does not say 'Velly nice flied lice' because he has some malformation of the tongue or palate. He says it because, for him, there is no important difference between l and r. These sounds are not important for him because the difference between l and r does not signal a difference between words in his language(s). It does, of course, in English, where the difference between lot and rot, for example completely depends on the difference between l and r. Since the

Chinese has no need to distinguish the two for his own language(s), he finds it difficult to do so when he has to speak English.

The basic items in the phonological system are *phonemes*. Phonemes are not the actual sounds made, but they are what the hearer perceives them as. The phoneme r will be perceived as r whether it is uttered by a bass Scot or a soprano Southerner. It is, in psychological terms, a *perceptual constant*, since it is extracted by the speaker from two such dissimilar sounds as the ones I have quoted. Phonemes are the basic units of phonology for each language. Some languages require more phonemes than others, but the point is that given its complete armoury of phonemes, every language contains all the sounds necessary to distinguish any word from any other word. Of course, some phonemes differ very little from each other; pat and bat differ only in that the p is unvoiced and the b is voiced. And there are some big differences in speech sounds which are not phonemic; contrast for example, a Londoner and a Yorkshireman saying path or class.

The phonemes of a language, then, are the basic phonological units of that language. In recent years, it has been shown that underlying the phonemes of each language are a set of *distinctive features*, which distinguish one phoneme from another. And it is probable that the same few distinctive features underlie the phonemes of all known languages. In our example pat and bat, the phonemes p and b are distinguished by only one distinctive feature, voiced or voiceless. Now consider the phonemes p and d; p is unvoiced while the d is voiced; and p is labial (made with the lips) while d is dental. These two phonemes, then, differ by at least two distinctive features. If you give people letters of the alphabet to remember, you find that they are more likely to confuse p and b than p and d. In other words, the more distinctive the letters the less likely we are to confuse them. We finish up with the startling fact that all the speech sounds in use can probably be analysed down to under a dozen distinctive features.

How is such a complex behaviour as language possibly derived from so few parts as phoneme and distinctive features?

The answer is that fifty-odd phonemes can be combined in many different ways – if you select any five at random, there are $5 \times 4 \times 3 \times 2 \times 1 = 120$ different orders in which those five might be arranged; and a dozen distinctive features, all allowing a binary (two-way) distinction to be made, can also be combined in different ways to give many different phonemes. We have arrived at the basic feature of language, what we can call its *productivity*. Out of a limited number of elements, an almost infinite number of combinations can be formed.

3 GRAMMATICAL SKILL

The second sub-skill is the *grammatical* one. Once again, the most obvious feature of grammatical skill is its productivity. Out of very few elements, so many different utterances can be constructed that some linguists are prepared to say that the number of sentences possible is infinite. What are the elements out of which sentences are constructed? We would probably reply words, but this is not strictly true. Sentences are composed of *morphemes*, which may be words or which may be smaller than words. For example, 'class' is a morpheme (whether uttered by a northerner or southerner). But 'classes' is two morphemes, 'class' plus the plural morpheme; so are 'classy', and 'classily'. These *inflexions* such as 'es' and 'ly', are very important, because they signal the function of the word of which they are part. The little *function words* such as 'the', 'is', and 'very', similarly signal the function of the word they precede. Indeed, the 'sentence' 'The erenstany cates elendied the edom eptly with ledear and aris' has a grammatical structure provided only by inflexion and function words.

This leads on to a most important point. It is not the identity of a word that is important in grammatical skill, but its *function*. The sentences 'The boy consumed the ice-cream', and 'The man purchased the car' contain different *content* words, but the words they contain have the same *functions*. They can in fact be described by certain 'parts of speech' or form classes, some of which we may have learned in grammar lessons at school. And so when a sentence is composed grammatically, we are in fact combining parts of speech, which are abstract elements, in a very large number of different possible orders.

Of course, there are limitations. In English, for example, one cannot say 'boy the', if one is using 'the' as the article to qualify 'boy'. And some of the regular combinations English requires are very complicated. Take the sentence 'Why didn't the milkman call today?' It is hardly surprising that children as old as five may say 'Why the milkman didn't call today?' This is because they expect the auxiliary verb 'did' to come close to the verb it qualifies, 'call', whereas in this particular combination of morphemes it has to be separated by a considerable distance.

It is very interesting that if a young child is given the task of saying the first word that comes into his head after the word you give him, e.g 'red', he will probably say 'shoes', whereas an adult is more likely to utter a word of the same form class (adjective) e.g. 'blue'. In other words, we may learn to organize the words we use in terms of the grammatical function they perform. In the case of grammatical, then, as in the case of phonological skill, there are abstract elements which we combine to form a vast number of possible combinations, and in both cases there are some combinations which are permitted and others which are not.

The word 'rules' is sometimes, rather misleadingly, used to describe the process of combining elements, or rather, of subdividing units and then combining the units that result from the subdivision. For there is evidence that when we *plan* a sentence grammatically, we start off with large-scale grammatical units, such as subject and predicate, and then fill in the grammatical details later. For example, we probably start planning the sentence 'The tall boy saved the drowning woman' with the boy as subject of the sentence and his saving of the woman as the predicate. But we do not supply the article 'the', the adjective 'tall', the inflexion 'ed', and the participle 'drowning' until later. You can imagine the amount of planning that is needed to transform the boy as the actor and his saving the woman as the action into such a sentence as 'The drowning woman was saved by the tall boy.'

c

4 SEMANTIC SKILL

Now we come to the skill of selecting morphemes and combining them in ways that make sense; this is *semantic* skill. The 'sentence' 'Colourless green ideas sleep furiously' is a regular and acceptable combination from a grammatical point of view, but the sense it makes is, to put it mildly, eccentric. There are an immense number of different combinations of morphemes which *do* make sense, but the combination above does not. Nor can one speak of inanimate objects such as stones thinking; of male organisms conceiving; or of counting mass nouns such as ink or rice. But the point is that semantic skill is *productive* in the same way as phonological and grammatical skill. Think, for example, of the number of possible two-word adjective–noun combinations consisting of colour adjectives and names of clothes.

It's interesting to note that semantic skills and experience of the world are closely related. One does not usually speak of a patient treating a doctor or a client advising a lawyer; but it is not clear to what extent this is because one has learned that the verb 'treated' is often used in combination with the word 'doctor' as the subject; and to what extent it is because one has experienced doctors as doing things to patients.

We have said that there are abstract elements (such as distinctive features and phonemes) which are the basis for the productive nature of phonological skill; and that grammatical features, such as subject and predicate, are similarly used as abstract elements from which other elements such as adjective or noun, are derived, and from which eventually a grammatical sequence is produced. What are the elements which underlie semantic skill?

One possibility is that we organize words in a hierarchical way; that is we organize them into groups, with sub-groups, with sub-sub-groups, etc. Thus we can quickly produce the words 'spaniel' and 'poodle' and 'bulldog' because we have them adequately stored and labelled by the class name 'dog'. In their turn, 'dog', 'cat', 'rabbit', etc. might be adequately grouped under such a heading as 'pets'; 'pets', 'farmyard animals', and 'wild animals' might be sub-sections under the label 'animals'; 'animals', 'humans', and 'plants' might be animate as opposed to inanimate objects, and so on. The benefits of such a system would be considerable, for it would enable a speaker trying to select a word to use to look under the right category label for it. For example, if he wanted to think of the word 'poodle', he would search under 'dog'; or, if he was not sure that it was a breed of dog he was looking for, he might start searching under the category label 'pet'. Such a system is obviously superior to a long list of words which the speaker has to search through as if through a dictionary before he comes to the one he wants. Even if he had such a list organized alphabetically, it is still a long search through all the ps before he comes to poodle.

The important advantage of a hierarchical system, then, is the speed of retrieval from the system. Another advantage is that there might be connections between different areas; for example, there might be connections between the system of which 'dog' is a part, and a system of verbs describing the noises made by animals and humans. In this case, there might be a constraint on one's choice of verb after using the word 'dog'; one could follow dog with the verb 'barks', but not with 'purrs'. Then one would know that all the words under the category 'dog' can be followed by 'bark'; poodles, spaniels and bulldogs bark.

Phonological, grammatical, and *semantic* sub-skills combine in language behaviour. As was stressed earlier, we don't need to employ them all to the full in a given situation. We seldom have to listen hard to particular speech sounds to see if they give the phoneme p or b, since we use the surrounding context to guess their identity. And we seldom have to hesitate to search for a word in the middle of a phrase when speaking, since we probably have quite a repertoire of ready-made and habitually used phrases available to us. In our example, 'Excuse me, could you tell me the time', the speaker probably uttered the phrase 'Excuse me' as a single item of speech – he did not need to put the words in order.

In other words, the description of the three sub-skills as separate is in a sense artificial. Indeed, it is 'artificial' experiments which control other sub-skills and concentrate on one which have made such descriptions possible. In everyday life, all three are involved together, and many psychologists are coming round to the common-sense conclusion that it is the *interpretation* of the message which the speaker intends and which the listener understands which is the most crucial point.

5 NON-LINGUISTIC SKILL

Most psychologists have ignored a fourth sub-skill of language behaviour, which from the teacher's point of view is perhaps the most important of all. This is the use of *non-linguistic context* of the utterance. The part this plays in communication has already been stressed (see p. 8). The *speaker's* utterance is considerably affected by the non-linguistic context. In the example 'The tall boy saved the drowning woman', 'tall' would not need to have been included in the sentence if there was only one boy on the beach. The teacher teaching conservation of number (see p. 15) may have to say, 'Now look at these red beads in a row and look at these other red ones in a row.' She will have to say this if there are other beads besides red ones in the tray; and if there are other beads which are not arranged in rows. If, in other words, there is a confused non-linguistic context (tray of beads), then the teacher will have to use a long sentence to reduce the child's uncertainty as to which ones she is talking about. But since it is development in thinking that the teacher is aiming for, then the language she uses should present as little difficulty as possible (see p. 15). Skill in the use of non-linguistic context when speaking means arranging the situation to permit the use of simple language behaviour to describe it; and it means using language in such a way as to direct attention to the vital feature of the environment.

Skill in using the non-linguistic context in *understanding* is similarly complex. The listener has both to use the language as a cue to which feature of the environment to attend to; and on occasion to use the non-linguistic context to help him understand the message. It is worth remembering that children may not pick out the same aspects of the environment as worth attention as does the teacher. The teacher may think that the only aspect of the tray of beads worth noting is their spatial arrangement – there are rows of beads of unequal length. But the child may concentrate on their colour, or on the fact that the random group of beads in the far corner of the tray looks like a face. So if there are beads on the tray other than those in the two rows necessary for teaching conservation of number, the teacher will have to use language to direct attention to the two rows first. Since her next task is to direct the child's attention away from the greater length of one row towards the act of counting, it is evident that it would have been far better to have removed the spare beads in the first place!

The previous example is from the field of teaching, but it is worth noting that there are social cues which help the production and the understanding of language. To use our example, 'Excuse me, but could you tell me the time', the person addressed is likely to guess that that is the question, since, in Britain anyway, there are not many other things that one says to a complete stranger.

6 LINGUISTIC SKILL

The reader may have noticed that throughout this discussion of language as skilled behaviour, the writer has assumed that the same principles underlie *perceiving* and understanding utterances as underlie *producing* and articulating them. This is a big claim to make, because, obviously, the one involves auditory and sometimes visual reception of messages, while the other involves the use of various speech organs to articulate and of auditory feedback to control articulation.

However, both production and reception are alike in that they are *active* processes. When receiving messages people actually impose structure on them. This was shown in the case of grammatical units by an interesting and novel experiment. Sentences were spoken to people, and in the middle of one of the words, a click was introduced. When asked afterwards where the click occurred, the subjects of the experiment misplaced it. They said that it occurred at the nearest grammatical break to the word in which it actually occurred. In other words, as they listened to the sentence, they were imposing structures on it so that the click was thought to have occurred between larger scale units. The same may be true of phonological features: there is some evidence to show that the same processes are used to recognize phonemes as are used to articulate the sounds which realize them.

Of course, there are differences between production and reception. The speaker often has an overall plan for an utterance which the hearer obviously cannot guess until he has heard a little of it. In the course of language development, understanding precedes production. And in the case of severely subnormal children, there is often specific damage to the brain or to the articulators which makes production particularly difficult. In general, though, the same principles, underlie both production and reception, a situation made possible by two basic factors.

The first is the *redundancy* of language (see p. 3). This means that there are a great many spare cues to help the listener impose the same structure of the utterance as the speaker used in planning it. If someone starts a sentence 'Those big boys . . .', there are two plurality cues, 'those' being plural and the morpheme 's' after 'boy'. What is more, there are four cues indicating that 'boys' is a noun – the two adjectives preceding it and the two plural features already mentioned. So the *listener* is helped by the redundancy to impose the structure the speaker intended. Redundancy helps the *speaker*, too. It enables him to remember the structures he has used in a sentence already; we are all familiar with people who cannot complete a sentence because they have forgotton what they started with. Furthermore, redundancy gives the speaker more time to search out the word or phrase he is searching for but cannot for the moment find.

The second factor which permits production and comprehension of messages to be controlled by the same principles is the complexity of the *brain*. We have seen that language skill is complex, and that like a computer, it involves the combination of few elements in many ways. We have also seen that language is planned in a hierarchical way (see p. 24). So we must suppose the existence of processes in the brain of a hierarchical nature, in order to regulate such behaviour.

These processes are probably largely *central* in nature; by that is meant that they will be partly independent of the processes which regulate particular senses or organs, for example, hearing or the articulatory organs. Thus the same central processes may regulate either perceiving and understanding or producing and articulating.

A word of caution must be entered here; we are not talking about the *content* of the brain, as though there were words, or abstract structures such as nouns or predicates literally in the brain. Nor are we implying that, when a speaker uses subject and predicate to structure his speech, he is conscious of doing so and can tell us that that is how he is speaking. We are merely saying that the behaviour of speaking and of listening is structured in certain ways, and that therefore the structures in the brain must resemble these structures if it is to direct such behaviour.

It is probable that the essential feature of these structures in the brain is their hierarchical nature. Many psychologists call them *schemata*. And there is no clear evidence leading us to believe that the processes in the brain regulating language behaviour are any different in kind from those regulating other behaviour, such as driving or problem solving. Putting it in terms of our definitions (see p. 14), thinking is probably basically no different from language.

The reader will probably have had enough of technicalities by now. This chapter has been nearly all psychological, with little application to teaching. However, if language is both a means of communication and a means of regulating thinking, then it seems essential to the teacher to understand its basic nature. Otherwise, she might think, for example, that the number of words a child can utter is a meaningful measure of his linguistic ability; or that all the errors a child makes are indicative of lack of linguistic skill. This last example makes it clear that we must also discuss the way children normally acquire their native language.

4 Language
Acquisition

1 PRODUCTIVITY

The rather controversial implication I made at the end of the
last chapter that not all the errors a child makes in his language
behaviour are indicative of lack of skill needs some explanation.
Take the words 'bringed' and 'mouses'. These are errors, in
the sense that the correct forms are 'brought' and 'mice'. But
the fact that they are virtuous errors becomes clear when we
consider how the child could have said such words. He almost
certainly did not remember them from someone else's utterance
and imitate them; for most of the mouses he has met will have
been called mice. He must have formed the word for himself by
adding 's' to the word 'mouse'. In other words, he has acquired
the regular rule that to form a plural you add 's' or 'es'. What
he has failed to do is to acquire the irregularities to this rule.
So one may conclude that at least up to the age of four, five, or
six, the word 'mouses' represents a virtuous error, in that it
indicates that the child has grasped the basic way of combining
plural morphemes with other morphemes.

Contrast the adult; if you say to an adult, 'Here is a man
glinging' (a nonsense word). 'Today he is glinging, but yester-
day he . . .?' The reply may be 'glinged', as it is in the case of
young children. But it may also be 'glang', 'glung', or 'glought'
(on the analogy of 'sang', 'clung', or 'brought'). The point I want
to make is that language acquisition does not concern the learning of the phonological, grammatical, or semantic items so much
as the learning of the acceptable ways of combining them. For
it is the *productive* quality of language which is the most vital
acquisition.

2 PHONOLOGICAL SKILL

We will take each sub-skill in turn, and see how modes of
combination of units develop. First, *phonological* skill. When

the child utters his first words, often somewhere around twelve months, a system is already implied. Suppose his first word is 'dada'. There are already two phonological units, the 'd' and the 'a'. Now suppose he says 'mama' and 'baba'. These words add two more units to the number available, and the three consonantal units can be substituted for each other to give the three words. So the child is already building up a *system* of elements and acceptable ways of combining them.

How has he acquired such a system? He has probably been acquiring it ever since he started to make different sounds on different occasions in a predictable way – comfort and discomfort sounds. Perhaps the distinction between open vowel and closed consonant was acquired during the cooing stage, while other distinctions may have been acquired during the babbling stage which follows it (about six to twelve months, but it varies). The babbling stage serves a very useful function, incidentally. When the child says 'dididi', or something similar, he is experimenting. He is making certain movements with his articulators, letting air out of his mouth in certain ways, and then using auditory feedback to see what effects these movements have.

So, by the time he utters his first word, the child has certain distinct units, some of them probably adult phonemes, at his disposal. Is he using the *distinctive features* (see p. 21) to distinguish them? Probably not; he is likely to be using all sorts of cues of his own instead, such as length of sound, its volume, its tone, and so on. These are probably the most noticeable features to him of the utterances he hears, so he takes them over and uses them to distinguish one sound from another.

How, then, does he acquire the distinctive features necessary to distinguish phonemes, for example, voiced versus voiceless? The answer may be that he gradually approximates more and more closely to the adult phonological system as he finds himself unable to make vital distinctions in his speaking or his listening. Phonemes are distinguished by distinctive features, and different words are distinguished by the different phonemes realized in them. So the communication requirements of production and reception of messages containing more and more different

words force the child to acquire the distinctive features of
adult speech.

There is a progression, then, from the child's own system
which he has derived from his experience of the most obvious
features of speech sounds through to the adult system. Such a
progression would require the processes of *assimilation and
accommodation* (see p. 8). The child assimilates adult utterances to his own system, but he has to accommodate his own
system when discrepancies between it and the systems of
others become apparent. The need to communicate, to ask for
one's needs or to please mother by following her instructions, provides strong motivation. The *order* in which the child acquires
adult phonemes may be affected by the importance of that phoneme for communication purposes; by its ease of perception ('p' distinguished from 'b' is late); or by its ease of
articulation ('r' distinguished from 'l' is late).

3 GRAMMATICAL SKILL

The same progression from an idiosyncratic system to a developed adult system is evident in the *grammatical* sub-skill.
Grammatical skill is evident as soon as children start putting
two words together (usually by around twenty-four months).
And even these earliest two-word utterances follow certain principles. Children use the two words to have different functions.
'This arm', 'This yellow', 'This pretty', 'This baby', are
examples of what are called pivot-open sentences. The pivot
word, 'This', occurs in the first position regularly, while the
second position is filled by various open class words within
the child's repertoire. These sentences are not reductions of
adult utterances, which simply miss out the less important
words; for the pivot word 'This' occurs far more often relative
to other words than it does in the adult utterances the child
hears.

So how does the child acquire the principle which enables
him to form sentences consisting of pivot plus open or open
plus pivot? One variable involved might be the *position* of a
word in adult utterances. The child might have noticed that the

word 'This' occurs in a regular position before a word it qualifies. A second candidate is the emphasis placed on certain words
by adults; if a word is spoken with particular stress, the child
might pay more attention to it in an important function for
himself. A third possibility is that the child forms classes of
words based on the situations in which they are used; for example
he might group together words his mother used when pointing
at things and naming them; or words which are used by her
when she is describing what she is doing; or words she uses to
prohibit his intended actions. It is clear that such classes of
words as these may form the basis for their later classification
into verbs, nouns, etc.

So, once again, the earliest examples of grammatical skill
are based on principles the child *imposes* on his utterances; and
these principles are based on those features of language to
which he pays most attention. As in the case of the phonological sub-skill, the child has gradually to approximate more
and more closely to the adult system. How does he do so?
Again, the answer may partly be the needs of the communication
situation; he needs to use more and more different examples of
a general type of construction, for example, the negative construction. Yet if he has to remember where to put the negative
morpheme in each of these examples, he has a terrible lot to
remember. It is far easier to learn the adult principles of forming
negative sentences, which take account of such things as
auxiliary verbs.

Examples should make this clearer. The three-year-old will
probably form all his negative sentences by putting the negative
at the front every time; e.g. 'No singing song', 'no play that',
'no fall'. However, he will soon need to put the negative morpheme elsewhere, for example if he is asking a question – 'Why
not go shops?' and auxiliary verbs such as 'is' or 'can' present
terrible difficulties, for the negative is supposed to follow them
('isn't', 'can't'), but precede the main verb ('He isn't coming
home'). One way out is to do what one four-year-old did, and
omit the auxiliary verb altogether – 'He not little, he big'.

It's clear, then, that so complicated a construction as the
negative throws a great strain on the child's own simple system,

and forces him to approximate more and more closely to adult principles. Since he needs to use the negative construction in different ways in order to achieve his communicative purposes, he has to change.

There are other reasons for development as well. There are all sorts of *cues* in language which point to the existence of classes of words or of larger constructions. The basic distinction of subject and predicate may become clear from sentences of regular affirmative form. These are the most common sort of sentence, and the subject comes first while what you have to say about it (the predicate) comes second. The form classes, such as noun or verb, are signalled by function words like 'this', 'the', 'that', 'those', and often by the plural morpheme tagged on to them (in the case of nouns); or by auxiliary verbs like 'is', 'will', 'has', preceding them and inflexions such as 'ing' or 'ed' following them (in the case of verbs). The child may learn to treat as a class those words which are regularly preceded and followed by the same morphemes.

One particular communication situation may aid the development of grammatical skill. It is called *expansion*. Suppose a child says 'Daddy gone work'; mother may reply 'Yes, Daddy's gone to work'. She has expanded what the child said by adding a function word and an inflexion. This is just the right sort of situation for accommodation to occur, since there is an obvious discrepancy between what the child just said and what the mother replied. Indeed, the child in his turn often imitates the mother's expansion; such imitation is not necessarily evidence of accommodation of schemata, but it certainly helps accommodation to occur.

4 SEMANTIC SKILL

We have described the idiosyncratic early grammatical skill, its origins, and the reasons for its gradual approximation to the adult grammatical system. Much less is known about the development of the *semantic* system. We have already said that it is not so much the number of words that are in the child's repertoire as the way they are organized.

However, let us first admit that the task of using a *single word* correctly is very complex. A Pekingese and a Great Dane are both dogs; but they differ so greatly in appearance that it is difficult to realize that the same name is appropriate for both of them. In order to be able to apply the name 'dog' correctly, the child has to be able to extract certain criterial features of 'doggyness' from all dogs. They bark, have four legs and a tail, are taken for walks on leads, etc. Of course, the only evidence that a child has acquired the correct use of the word is his use of it to describe a novel instance of the class dog, one that he has never seen before. If the animal he calls a dog is the mongrel from next door, he may merely be remembering that that particular animal has been called 'dog' in his hearing.

This is a point of general application to teachers; it is easy to learn a label for an object, and that is what the child will do if you have already shown him a square, named it for him, and then asked him what it is. If, however, he can recognize a larger square and a smaller square, a red square and a black square, a square house and a square room as squares, and a circle, a triangle and rectangle as not-squares, then one can be confident that he has acquired the correct use of the word. So obviously, the acquisition of the meaning of 'content' words like dog involves connections between thinking and language. Specifically, it involves perceiving an animal in such a way as to extract from the whole situation a few crucial features.

However, the word 'dog' is hardly typical. It is a word used for reference to a particular class of object, and we have noted previously (see p. 13) that there are many, many words which are not used to refer either to objects in the world or to 'concepts in the mind'. How does the child acquire a semantic *system* which enables him to use these words acceptably *in combination*? Probably through noting the words with which they occur. Take the words 'down' and 'during'. The child hears the phrases 'during the day' or 'during dinner-time', but never 'down the day' or 'down dinner-time'; he hears 'down the stairs' or 'down the road', but never 'during the stairs' or 'during the road'. So 'down' is used of position, 'during' of time, since the words with which they are used are position or time words. Clearly, such learning can only occur if these latter words are already within the child's repertoire, so there *is* a sense in which it is important to have a wide repertoire of certain words. Relational words, such as prepositions, can only be acquired in this way, since they must be used of the relationship of known items to each other. The best way of teaching prepositions, of course, is to keep the related objects the same and vary only the relationship – The car is going over, under, round, through, by, along, the bridge.

One source of semantic skill, then, is the way in which words are used *together* in utterances which the child hears. In fact, this is closely connected with grammatical skill. If someone says 'Sometimes I go running down the road knocking on people's doors', then the fact that the child can treat 'down the road' as a phrase means that he can recognize that 'down' primarily qualifies 'road'; therefore he can learn that 'down' goes with 'place' words.

Moreover, the hearing of words used together (for example, 'down the road') does not only help the child to use the word *'down'* correctly, that is, qualifying 'place' words. It also helps him to treat the *place words* as being related to each other. They are all qualified by the word 'down', and also by certain other prepositions such as 'up' and 'along', and these prepositions act as clues to suggest that the words they qualify are related. We suggested in the previous chapter (see p. 24) that the important thing was the way words are organized into classes, sub-classes, and so on. This organization may develop in just such a way as has been suggested; for example, the adult will talk a lot on a visit to the zoo of feeding the monkeys, the elephants, etc. This might lead to a class of things one feeds, and indeed, the adult may provide a label for the class by speaking in general of feeding the animals. It has been shown that when children as young as four and five are given a list of items to remember presented to them in random order, they will remember them with the related items together.

The development of the semantic system, then, is very complex. Once again, idiosyncratic systems give way to conventionally accepted ones. At the younger ages all sorts of strange things happen even to the use of a single word, let alone words in sequence. For example, the word 'quah' was first used of a duck on a pond. It was then used of the water in a glass and of the milk in a bottle. Next it was used of an eagle on a coin, then of many round (coin-like) objects. In other words, the child used the word 'quah' to refer to whatever aspect of the situation he was paying attention to. First, perhaps in imitation of an adult, to a duck; then to liquids; then to birds in general; then to round things in general. The use of the word, in other words, was haphazard partly because the child's selection of features of the environment was also haphazard. Even when individual words are used correctly, they may not be used correctly together. For example, many children speak of inanimate objects such as chairs or plates, having feelings or performing actions which are in the range of humans only. Later they approximate more closely to the semantic rules of adults, but still permit plants and trees to feel sad. Is it experience of life or experience of language which leads to this development?

5 AN OVERVIEW

In the three major sub-skills of language behaviour, then, we find the same overall pattern. Children notice certain features of language behaviour, and use these features to form their own individual system of combination. However, the needs of communication, the requirement for more words and more complex ways of combining them, force them to approximate more and more to adult systems. So, of course, does the need to be understood by a variety of other people. When his only communicant is his mother or his twin, the child may be held back by baby language. But as soon as he needs to speak to other members of the community, the rules of the conventional code of language become more necessary.

The account I have given is at variance with a currently popular view of how language is acquired. This account assumes that the child is born with certain basic linguistic skills *preprogrammed into his brain*. All that needs to occur is that the child hears language uttered; this will activate these innate structures, and enable the child to use the basic rules from the start. How otherwise, ask some scientists, can the astonishing speed of acquisition and the new utterances the child creates be explained? This theory is based on the dubious assumption that human beings have specific systems pre-programmed in the brain. An analogy is made with the chick, who will follow the first moving object it encounters after emerging from the egg as if it were its mother; or the young gull, who will scuttle for shelter when the wing-shape of a bird of prey is placed in view, but not when the wing-shape of another bird is shown, even though it has seen neither before.

However, there is no evidence that human beings are specific in this way. True, in adults and adolescents, the processes which regulate language are in most cases situated in the left hemisphere of the brain; but in the very early years, the brain is very plastic. By that I mean that other parts of the brain can take over functions served by a part which has been injured. A more likely account suggests that as the brain develops, more complex ways of regulating behaviour become possible, in particular, hierarchical as opposed to sequential strategies. By this I mean that the structures in the brain permit overall plans to be made because they are hierarchical in nature, rather than merely letting one piece of behaviour lead to another. If this is the case, there is no reason to suppose that language behaviour is regulated by different processes to other behaviour; language and thinking need not be different in kind.

Although a child may have fairly well developed language skills, it does not necessarily follow that he can *communicate* adequately. As we have seen, successful communication required fitting the utterance to the non-linguistic context and to the listener. Suppose one blindfolds an adult, and then brings him into the room and tells a six-year-old to direct him to pick up an object from the corner of the room; the child will probably say 'Go over there and pick it up'. In other words, he hasn't taken into account the communication requirements of the listener, who does not know where 'there' is or what 'it' is. Similarly, a child will solve a problem involving the workings of a mechanism after verbal instruction, but he will be quite unable to explain to another child how to do so. Comprehension precedes production in a child's development.

6 IMPLICATIONS

The implications of this chapter for the teacher are considerable. Limiting ourselves to language acquisition and leaving thinking out of consideration, the major point to be made is that children only acquire skills by practising them. Thus they acquire the skills of language behaviour only by engaging in it. Secondly, such practice should occur in a variety of meaningful contexts. The child should be engaged in behaviour which requires the use of language to ensure its success. Thirdly, language behaviour should not be corrected in the sense that a child is told that he has made a mistake. As we have seen, many mistakes are virtuous mistakes in that they indicate that a certain point of development has been reached. Rather, the child should be answered in such a way that the teacher uses correctly and apparently naturally in reply the construction or word which the child got wrong. It is very easy for a teacher to raise a laugh by ridiculing a child's error in pronunciation, grammar, or choice of words. Such ridicule reveals only the teacher's poverty of self-esteem and lack of sensitivity. Finally, and most important, it is modes of combination of words which are more important, not the words themselves. It is far more important to be able to use constructions in different situations than to be able to name uncommon objects. For constructions enable one to describe complex relations in the real world, such as cause and effect ('If I do this, then this will happen'); and to regulate behaviour in complex ways.

Just in case this last point has been misunderstood, I am not suggesting that children should be *taught grammar* in the sense that they should be taught that this word is a noun, this a verb, etc. Such an analysis of one's own behaviour demands an advanced level of thinking (operational thinking, see p. 55). What I am suggesting is that the teacher should provide situations in which the child has to use more complex constructions in order

D

to communicate adequately. Anyway, why should any knowledge of grammatical terms help the child's language development? He has long ago mastered structures of a far greater complexity than noun and verb without knowing what to call them or even being aware that he is using them.

5 Language Deficit and Remediation

1 ENVIRONMENTAL DEPRIVATION – ITS NATURE

If language is necessary for the public task of communicating and the private task of regulating one's own behaviour, then it is important that language skills should be adequately acquired. The previous chapter presented a picture of the development of language which implied that development was almost predetermined. True, human beings have evolved as language-using organisms; but the environment in which the language skills develop is also of great importance. Both *maturation* (physiological development) and *experience* are necessary, and interference with either factor results in language deficit.

There are various specific conditions which result in impaired language skills. These will be considered briefly later in the chapter, since their remediation is a job for specialists. However, there are also deficits in children's experience which lead to language deficit. This *environmental deprivation* is often termed cultural deprivation. Its existence has been officially recognized by the setting up of educational priority areas; but the specific variables which cause language deficit are only just emerging from the research.

Research shows that the language skills of working-class children are less developed than those of middle-class children. In this type of research, class is usually defined by the occupation of the child's father. Obviously, it would be ridiculous to infer that the working-class children are less developed linguistically because their fathers work with their hands. We must look for particular features of working-class life which affect linguistic development.

First, however, it is necessary to consider what the deficits actually are. The differences found have been described in terms of different *codes* of language. The working-class is considered to have only a *restricted* code available, but the middle-class possess both a restricted and an *elaborated* code. However, all the differences which have been discovered experimentally have been differences of degree rather than differences of kind. For example, when working-class and middle-class youths discussed subjects such as capital punishment in groups, the following results were among those obtained: the middle-class youths used longer sentences; their sentences were more grammatically complex, in that they used more subordinate clauses; they used more qualifiers, for example, adverbs and adjectives; and their vocabulary was wider, as indicated by the ratio of the total number of words they used to the number of different words.

The differences between the social classes is thus a matter of degree; working-class children are at a disadvantage, particularly in *grammatical* skills. Investigations of younger children show that working-class three- and four-year-olds use much larger units as grammatical items. Grammatical skill in middle-class children involves the ordering of morphemes; but in working-class children of the same age it involves the ordering of groups of morphemes. The working-class child, in other words, has a limited number of phrase-sized units, and therefore many fewer combinations of items are open to him. For example, he may say 'That big dog' as a single unit, having to miss out the auxiliary 'is' and the article 'a' in order to remember it all. This sentence is a unit for him, and so he has to say 'That big dog, that little dog' if he wishes to compare dogs. For the middle-class child, however, the morphemes are the units he orders grammatically; so he can say 'That's a big dog, but this isn't', or 'Isn't that a big dog?' or 'That's a big dog, isn't it?'

These differences in skill do not constitute 'different languages'. But they are important when language behaviour is used for certain *purposes*. In a discussion of capital punishment, for example, language behaviour is used to analyse the arguments of others and put forward one's own in a consistent way. Indeed, grammatical skill is necessary for the verbal expression of any logically coherent analysis.

Since academic secondary education demands such expression, it seems clear that children who are handicapped in linguistic skills will be handicapped *academically*. Language is also used to regulate behaviour and thinking. Therefore linguistic retardation may affect the logical thinking required in academic subjects as well as the communicative expression (see Chapter 6). However, it has been shown that groups from different social classes which differ markedly in linguistic skills differ little when tested on a non-verbal intelligence test. Perhaps the conclusion might be that the primary effect of linguistic retardation is on communicative skill; since academic performance is often judged on the basis of communicative skill, the effect of linguistic retardation on academic performance may be exaggerated. If one defines academic performance in terms of the thinking processes required to solve problems, then the effect of linguistic retardation is less clear. As will be seen in the next chapter, language has an effect on thinking, but the relation is complex and the effect limited.

2 ENVIRONMENTAL DEPRIVATION – ITS CAUSES

Which variables in the experience of culturally deprived children lead to linguistic deprivation? The early and basic 'lessons' of language are learned from the child's mother. Are there, then, any features of the *modes of communication* of working-class mothers with their children which could cause language deficit? One obvious possibility, of course, is that the mother's own language skills are under-developed. Another is that the mother may use language to control the child's behaviour, rather than to comment on a situation or answer questions about it. Language behaviour used to control behaviour on the child's part is largely a one-way communication situation. There is certainly little feedback of a verbal kind, either from the child to the parent or vice versa. Contrast the situation where the child comments on a situation or asks a question; the mother has the chance to reply, expanding what the child said (see p. 34). Two-way communication is clearly an ideal situation for learning language skills.

As the working-class child grows older, he may find that other modes of communication are required of him. One situation in particular may be typical of much of his experience. This is the situation where a group of people or a couple of people talk in order to reinforce their *solidarity* with each other. The term solidarity is not used in a political sense so much as in a social or emotional sense. People frequently use language to indicate that they share the same assumptions, values, and experiences as each other. Much is left unexpressed that might formally be expressed, and phrases such as 'you know' and 'isn't it' imply common experience and assume assent. Obviously, such a communication situation does not encourage individual analysis of or dissent from the shared assumptions; this analysis on the individual's part, the standing outside a situation and looking objectively at it, is at a premium in academic education.

3 STRATEGIES OF REMEDIATION

If language skills depend on experience as well as on natural development, then they can be consciously taught. How, then can the deficits due to cultural deprivation be remedied? One approach has been to *enrich* the child's experience. Children have been taken on outings to such places as zoos, docks, railway terminals, and museums. They have been encouraged to talk and write about their experiences when they returned to school. Enriched experience required enriched language to describe it adequately. But the implication is that the experience itself somehow provides the basic source of language improvement. This is theoretically unlikely, and in practice results have been disappointing.

As a reaction against these rather non-specific methods, it has recently been proposed to use much more *formal* methods of instruction. These methods use language behaviour on the teacher's and the children's part which is used outside any non-linguistic context. In other words, they are not talking about what they are doing or how they are feeling. Rather, they are engaged in language drills. These drills are based on what is known about language development as analysed by linguists; since linguists analyse language abstracted from its context, the drills ignore the context. As a result, skills so acquired may not generalize to any situation other than that of instruction. Further, unless the teacher is very skilful, motivation may be difficult to sustain.

The alternative to the two strategies quoted above is to have *specific aims* in teaching; for example, one wishes the child to master comparatives and superlatives, regular and irregular (big, bigger, biggest; good, better, best); and to approach these aims by small and carefully programmed steps. Thus the best points of the drills are retained. On the other hand, the situations in which the language teaching occurs should be the *normal context* of the construction being taught. This is important, first, because language is learned in the first place in context; and second, because it is motivating to use language for a purpose, particularly if that purpose is itself interesting.

Another benefit of this approach is that it allows training in both *comprehension* and *production* of language. Comprehension occurs before production in the normal development of language, and therefore it is advisable to ensure that the construction being taught is comprehended before production (utterance) is demanded. Comprehension, it will be remembered, required no verbal response, but merely behaviour which indicates that the child has understood. For example, the children could have a series of objects of different size, and be required to hold up one in response to the question, 'Show me the biggest one.' Obviously, a context of utterance (in this case, objects of differing size) is required before comprehension can be taught or tested.

A final benefit of the use of a non-linguistic context is that it enables different *uses* of language to be taught. Younger children will need specific training in different grammatical constructions, but older children will also need to learn different sorts of language behaviour (registers, see p. 78) to use on different occasions. For example, the language behaviour appropriate to expressing a boy's feelings after finishing with a girl is different in many ways from that appropriate to an interview for a job. As has been mentioned earlier in this chapter, the use of language behaviour in reinforcing a group's solidarity is different from that appropriate to expressing a personal analysis or opinion.

4 TACTICS OF REMEDIATION

It is not usually possible for teachers to engage in a one-to-one language teaching situation with a child. Such a situation would of course be ideal; it parallels nature's 'teaching' situation of mother and child. Neither does it seem realistic to suggest language teaching for the class as a unit. Firstly, participation by all members of a class is notoriously hard to achieve; and secondly, different children may be at very different stages of language development. Work in *groups* of four or five can bring together children of the same level of language development; further, two equivalent groups allow the possibility of competition between groups.

The principle, then, is to tailor the teaching programme to linguistic development level, treating children of roughly the same level together in groups. The first problem, obviously, is to discover at what *level* a child is. Theoretically, observation and testing of each individual child should reveal his level. However, practically speaking, all that the teacher may be able to do is to divide the children in his class into good, moderate, and poor on the basis of his general impressions of their language skills. These ratings will be relative to the class; it is too much to expect the teacher to be able to make judgements relative to the norm in the child population as a whole. However, this discussion presupposes that the teacher has decided that the class needs specific language instruction, and this decision *will* be taken as a result of comparison with what might be expected of children of a similar age. However, this decision will not be too difficult, since very many factors will indicate to the teacher that his class comes in general from culturally impoverished homes.

Having formed groups of children based on rough judgements of linguistic competence, the next problem is – *What to teach*? One might try to teach different language constructions to the different groups, on the grounds that the more advanced child-

ren should have mastered, for example, comparatives and superlatives by now. However, there are different levels of difficulty
within constructions. Take comparatives and superlatives; it
will be easier to select the biggest from three similar items than
from seven dissimilar items; and it will be harder to select the
bigger of two items when it was previously the smaller of another pair than when no such prior pairing had occurred. It is
unlikely that all children in the class will have completely
mastered any given construction. So the teaching tactic best
suited to this situation may be to set the groups to work at
different levels of difficulty within the same construction.

Which construction should one teach? If the need for language instruction is recognized in the school, it will be possible to
start with the five-year-old intake. Ideally, language instruction
should start much earlier even than this. If one does start with
the reception class infants, then simple constructions such as
prepositions and simple qualifiers should be taught. These
refer to spatial relationships ('over the bridge', 'under the bridge')
or clearly defined features of objects ('red ball', 'blue ball').
More complex constructions come later, with verb tenses,
comparatives and superlatives, 'if . . . then' implication, and the
correct use of 'all', 'some' or 'none', proving harder. Finally
correct use of the various sentence types, interrogative, negative,
imperative, and passive proves very difficult. Particularly hard
are the combinations of these, e.g. 'Why wasn't the postman
bitten by the dog this morning?' (interrogative + negative +
passive). Fortunately, such complex constructions are rarely used.

What *teaching methods* should be used? If the need to teach
comprehension before production is recognized, there are several
alternatives. The teacher can, for example, provide material for
two groups in competition at any given level. They might have
in front of them items of different size, density, brightness.
Then the teacher might ask a question, 'Bring me the biggest'
or 'softest'. Such a situation not only teaches grammatical
comprehension of superlatives, but also semantic dimensions
of size, texture, and brightness.

The teaching of *production* will be harder, for obvious practical reasons. One possibility might be to place a barrier between

a pair of children and then tell child A to instruct child B to perform an operation with some material which A has already learned. If, for example, the task is to roll a car of a certain colour in a certain direction, A will have to use the qualifier 'red' to distinguish the requisite car from the others which B has in front of him; and he will have to use prepositions to indicate the required route. Pointing and other gestures have been made impossible, so language behaviour is the only means of communication available.

These are merely specific practical hints. The *principles* involved are the same as those involved in any teaching. Programme the teaching in *steps* which differ only slightly in difficulty. And vary the task to ensure that *generalization* to other situations will take place. For example, when teaching comparatives, use regular forms to start with (e.g. big, bigger, biggest). But use different words within the same semantic dimension (size) (e.g. large, larger, largest); and use different semantic dimensions too (e.g. texture-soft, softer, softest). Later, start employing irregular forms, and later still phrases rather than words (e.g. 'Show me the ball which is bigger'). Use objects which differ considerably in size to begin with, but later which differ less; use the same object to begin with (e.g. 'Which is the bigger *ball*?') preferably employing balls which differ only in size; later use balls of differing colours; and later still, different objects altogether. Only by planning instruction in small steps but with considerable variety within each step will *generalized* learning of *principles* of language rather than isolated learning of individual words occur.

A final problem, of course, is how to assess whether the stated *aim* (in this example, the comprehension and production of comparatives and superlatives) has been reached. This information is vital as feedback to teacher and pupil. The only course open seems to be some more formal situation in which each child makes a personal response to a question. To test comprehension, the teacher may ask the same form of question as we have discussed already (e.g. 'Show me the biggest ball'). To test production, the teacher has to prompt. One method is for the teacher to say the first part of a sentence himself (e.g. 'Look,

Bill, here's a long train, but here's an even . . .' raising the pitch of his voice). The teacher will have to decide for himself what level of test performance he will accept as indicating mastery of the construction. But the major feature of any such post-instruction test is that it should test new instances (examples) of the construction being taught. For example, the 'long train' quoted above should not have been employed in the teaching phase, only in the test phase.

Remediation at the *secondary* school level should usually employ the social situations in which language behaviour is used rather than with the physical objects or events to which it sometimes refers. In fact, however, the transition from 'object bound' language teaching to 'social situation' language teaching may partly occur at primary school. For in the teaching of the production of the more complex sentence types, social situations are ideal for making the use of such sentences necessary. An information-seeking situation (asking the way) stimulates inter-rogatives; an authority situation (telling younger children what to do) stimulates imperatives. Social situations which may be employed at the secondary level include interviews and other such cases where language behaviour of a certain type, de-signed to meet the communicative needs of the situation, is appropriate.

However, the area of language behaviour which most needs remediation at the secondary stage is not its social but what we may call its *academic* use; that is, the use of language outside a concrete or a social context to analyse and evaluate. Unfortun-ately the child may see the academic task as in fact a social use of language – the sort of utterance or writing which the teacher wants or expects. However, this merely indicates that he has not grasped the basic requirement of the situation – analysis rather than obligation.

Tentative suggestions for language training at this stage include the playing of roles which demand description and explanation of a situation. These roles should have in common the need to stand outside a situation and analyse it. They might be graded in terms of the degree of abstraction involved in explanation, for example, from commentator's description of a football match, through critic's analysis of a film, to scientist's explanation of a phenomenon (e.g. rate of swing of a pendulum, see p. 57). It is worth noting, however, that adequate use of language in this way may depend on the attainment of a certain stage of thinking (see p. 58). This raises the wider educational issue – to what extent should the academic use of language be required in schools?

5 SPECIFIC LANGUAGE DEFICIT

This section deals briefly with language disorders due primarily to variables other than cultural deprivation. The discussion will be brief because the treatment of these deficits is a job for a specialist. The *recognition* that a child might have such a deficit, however, may be the teacher's task. Referral to the specialist to discover whether her suspicion is justified is the next step. Only when assessment reveals the existence and precise nature of the deficit will treatment be undertaken.

The first type of deficit involves specific impairment of the *mechanisms* of speaking. For example, stammering is, in effect, poor co-ordination of respiration and voicing; articulation can be affected by abnormality in those parts of the brain which regulate movement of tongue, lips, teeth or palate; and articulation can also be affected by abnormalities of those organs themselves.

A second type of deficit consists of disorders resulting from *other specific conditions*. Hearing loss, mental subnormality, or psychiatric disorder (or combinations of these three), very often result in deficits. These deficits are not only of articulation, but may also involve the production and understanding of language behaviour.

A third type of deficit has only recently been recognized. It is termed *developmental speech disorder*, and refers to gross delays in language development which cannot be attributed to any other condition. Some children are merely late developers; others may retain the handicap throughout childhood. One way of attempting to spot this type of deficit early is to refer for further examination all children who are not putting words together by the age of three.

A final type of deficit is termed acquired *dysphasia*. This term refers to the loss of speech or language functions which have already been acquired. This loss is due to specific brain damage as a result of injury or illness.

It is the third type of disorder which the teacher is most likely to spot; the others are more likely to have been noticed already. Research shows that children with developmental speech disorders are apt to have been later in standing and walking than normal. They are also likely to have been later in establishing left- or right-handedness, and to have poor co-ordination of their movements. Finally, they are apt to be excessively distractible, and they come from families where there are more multiple births (twins, triplets) than average.

In many cases, there may be more than one of these four types of deficit present. Clearly, many of the conditions which cause language deficit are not curable. Therefore the main hope for improvement lies in remediation of language behaviour. The nature of the remediation employed obviously depends on the nature of the deficit. For example, speech therapists are especially concerned with disorders of articulation.

A first step, however, is to discover the areas of language behaviour in which the child is particularly deficient. This is done by means of psychological tests which test different aspects of language skill. A profile can then be drawn up indicating those particular areas in which a child is deficient. Deficiency is defined in terms of the extent to which the child's score is below the average score obtained on that part of the test by a large sample of children of the same age.

Techniques of remediation for articulatory disorders are fairly advanced, but are at a very crude stage in the case of grammatical and semantic disorders. Since trained personnel are so few, instruction to mothers on how to stimulate language development in their children is an urgent necessity.

6 Language
and Thinking

I LANGUAGE AND THINKING

First I should like to repeat our *definitions* of the terms language and thinking. We use language to refer to the processes in the brain which regulate language behaviour, and thinking to denote the processes which regulate non-verbal behaviour. So to discuss the relations between language and thinking is to discuss the relation between processes in the child's brain.

There are two basic approaches to the problem among psychologists. Some say that language is a necessary condition of thinking; thinking is impossible without language. Others maintain that language aids thinking, but is not a necessary condition. In fact, both groups are using terms of such generality that clear-cut answers are impossible. For as we have seen, language develops as the child matures; and thinking, too, develops, passing through stages which differ in kind from each other.

So the sort of questions which ought to be asked are more specific and are developmental in nature; one might ask, for example, whether the development of certain grammatical skills makes it more likely that certain logical skills may also develop. Alternatively, one might ask questions implying that a certain stage of thinking is a necessary condition of language; for example, one might ask, does the child have to have reached the stage of conservation (see p. 56) before he can use accurately comparative words such as 'more'? The terms used of stages of thinking will be more adequately defined later. The point I am trying to make is that the questions to be put about language and thinking are *developmental* questions; can certain uses of language hasten the development of stages of thinking? Does the development of a certain stage of thinking make certain types of language behaviour possible?

2 INTERNALIZATION

However, before one can answer these questions, one has to ask how language and thinking could have become related in the first place. The answer is probably in terms of the process we call *internalization*. The first step is for the *language behaviour of someone else* (for example his mother) to affect the child's behaviour, and therefore his thinking. For example, the mother may say 'Go and see John', and the child obeys. She may say 'Don't use your fingers', and the child may stop pushing his food in with his hands. In both cases, she has affected his behaviour by her own language behaviour, in the first case to activate behaviour and in the second to inhibit it. So what has happened is that the child has understood a message and changed his behaviour accordingly.

The next stage in internalization is for the child to use *his own language behaviour* to regulate his other behaviour. In other words, he tells himself out loud what to do. Children aged three, four, and five in particular, engage in this egocentric speech. They are not intending to communicate because quite often they use egocentric speech when they are completely alone; often, they are directing their play.

The final stage is to inhibit the language behaviour and use *language*, the *process*, to regulate behaviour. It should be stressed that it is not necessarily sentences or words that are internalized. Rather, it is the processes in the brain which normally regulate language which are being used to regulate other behaviour. Some indication of this is given at late periods in the second stage of internalization. By then the child has inhibited almost all his language behaviour, but a little still remains; what does remain is often the logical object of his actions, e.g. 'bricks', or perhaps, the verb, e.g. 'build', indicating in a word what he has to do. In other words, it is the basic grammatical features which are the last to be internalized; so perhaps it is the grammatical and semantic processes which regulate them which are being used to regulate the non-verbal behaviour.

The complete internalization of language may have occurred

in many five-, six-, and seven-year-olds. Of course, this does not mean that thinking cannot occur adequately until then. Several stages of thinking have already been passed through by this age. What it does mean, however, is that a child has a very powerful *tool* at his disposal. Before internalization, at the first stage, it is his mother who uses language to regulate his behaviour. She directs his attention to various objects or events by naming them; she controls which words are used of which objects, thereby affecting his own word classes; and, above all, she manipulates his behaviour by telling him what he has to do and what object he has to do it to.

How different it is at the second and third stages. By now the child can use his own language to regulate his behaviour. The feature of language which has been stressed throughout this book so far is its productivity. Using few elements, one can produce many different combinations. So, *theoretically*, the child should be able to regulate his behaviour in a multitude of different and novel ways; not only may Mummy smack Martin, but Martin smack Mummy! What's more, the child is not tied to the present. He can use language to refer to items or events not present, and thus he can manipulate them in anticipation (that is, he can plan ahead).

However, it is not quite so simple as this. For language and thinking may not connect in the easy way suggested. The processes of language and those of thinking may be at different stages of development, and language may have to wait for thinking to catch up.

3 IMPLICATIONS OF INTERNALIZATION

Nevertheless, the process of internalization has important implications for teaching. Suppose a teacher is trying to instruct a child how to draw a person. She says 'Now, what's your Daddy got, Billy? He's got a head and a body and legs and arms and hands and feet, hasn't he? And he's got a face, too hasn't he? Now, you draw your Daddy for me.' Her instructions are aimed at helping the child to produce a father, or any other human figure, with the appropriate appendages. But if the child is directing his behaviour by *her* language behaviour, he has a very difficult task. For he has to remember what she said while he is drawing each part of the body. (The teacher, of course, has moved on.)

Suppose, however, that he can direct his task by *his own* language behaviour, aloud. In this case, he can tell himself what to do. 'Now, what has my daddy got? He's got a head. How does his head go? The eyes go here . . .' and so on. The use of his own language behaviour enables him to break the task down as he does it. More important, it is a step towards complete internalization. It is a step teachers often miss out, assuming that children go straight from being told a few times how to do a thing to doing it without being told. Telling themselves how to do it out loud is perhaps a vital intermediate step in the sequence. In our example, the teacher, having given his instructions, could have asked the child to tell him back *in his own words* how he was going to do the task. At least, by these means, the teacher would know that the child understood his instructions; and that he had available language behaviour which he could use to regulate his drawing behaviour.

4 THE DEVELOPMENT OF THINKING: OPERATIONAL
  THINKING

However, once language has been internalized, we have to discover points of development at which language and thinking can interact; and this interaction has to be such that the language is not too complex in structure to regulate the processes of thinking. Our next step, therefore, must be to discuss the development of thinking from this point of view. I am not going to give an overall account of cognitive development, but am merely going to stress particular transitions from one stage of development to the next. This should make clear those features of the subsequent stage which may permit language to play a part which it could not play in the previous stage.

The major transition with which we are concerned is that between *pre-operational and operational thinking*, occurring around six to eight years. The main difference between these two

E

stages is in the way in which the child represents to himself his environment and behaviour. In the pre-operational stages, the child uses *images* to represent his environment and regulate his behaviour. This does not mean that he has a photographic record of objects or events, but rather that he has abstracted certain features of the situation from which he can recreate it for himself if necessary. For example, his image of dog will consist of the features he has abstracted (see p. 35).

In the operational stages of thinking, on the other hand, the child uses *symbols* rather than images. By symbols are meant processes which *stand for* aspects of the environment or of behaviour. Symbols can be manipulated so that their order is completely changed. Note that this is not the case with the parts of the image, which must be 'put back together again' in the same order. Nevertheless, symbols may not be manipulated in any way whatever. There are constraints, rules of implication, which limit the set of possible recombinations. Nevertheless, with the number of symbols available and the number of rules permissible, there is an immense number of different combinations possible.

The experiments on *conservation* illustrate the difference between the stages of operational and pre-operational thinking. Two balls of Plasticine are shown to the child, and he agrees that there is the same amount of Plasticine in each. One is then rolled out into a sausage shape, and the child is asked whether there is more, less, or the same amount in the sausage as in the other ball. The pre-operational child will say that there is more or less; this is one aspect of the way in which his perception of the situation has dominated his thinking. The operational child, however, uses symbols to represent behaviour. He can therefore *reverse* the order of symbols representing the rolling out of the first ball into the sausage shape; the sausage, he sees, can become a ball again, the same ball as before. So he is able to say that there is the same amount in the sausage as in the second ball. This success is achieved by the rule-governed manipulation of symbols, the rule in this case being the rule of reversibility; that an operation performed and then performed in reverse leads to the same situation as one started with.

The similarity of operational thinking to mature language is immediately evident. For language, too, involves the manipulation of items according to rules, but allowing a vast number of possible combinations. Both language and operational thinking, in other words, are *productive*. Perhaps there are even similarities between some of the rules which govern language and some of those which govern thinking. On the face of it, then, the period of transition to operational thinking is the ideal opportunity for connections to be founded between language as a system and thinking. For at this stage, both language and thinking are of comparable complexity.

5 THE DEVELOPMENT OF THINKING: CONCRETE AND FORMAL OPERATIONS

The other major transition between stages which might be of importance in this context is the transition at around eleven to fifteen between two sub-stages of operational thinking, *concrete* and *formal*. The difference between these two sub-stages is that in formal operations, a limited set of symbols is used; representation is in terms of a *closed system* of symbols, so certain operations are possible which are not possible in concrete reasoning. For example, all other variables in a situation may be kept constant, and one varied. Thus different hypotheses can be tested by varying different variables. In such cases, it will be noticed, there are second-order relations; that is, there are relations not only between the variables but also between the hypotheses, since one hypothesis might rule out another.

An example of a formal reasoning problem is to determine the cause of the rate of swing of a pendulum. Does it go faster or slower depending on the weight on the end, the length of the string, or the point from which you let it fall? There are no other alternative variables apparent, so there is a closed system of alternatives. There are several hypotheses possible, involving variables singly and in combination. For example, it might be pendulum length, or it might be a mixture of length and weight, which determines rate of swing. Formal operational thinking, then, permits formal logical inferences to be made because it is a closed system. Once again the part which language could play is clear. The language system might suggest possible modes of combination of variables and possible logical relations which the symbol system might not yet have used. Further, it will enable alternative hypotheses to be labelled and stored in memory.

Now one must ask, what precisely is the relationship of language and thinking at these two crucial transitions between stages of thinking? Psychologists are not in agreement. Many would say that the stages in cognitive growth are largely determined by a combination of maturation and non-linguistic experience, but language cannot hasten the onset of any stage. Once a stage has been reached, however, development within that stage may well be accelerated by additional language instruction from an adult (and therefore by activation of the child's own language). This point of view is perhaps supported by the finding that deaf children, who certainly do not have a normal experience of language, are only a little behind normal children in the development of their thinking. So there follows the conclusion that language *in its fully productive capacity* is not connected with thinking until thinking becomes operational.

What then would be the point of a lot of linguistic instruction in tasks demanding operational thinking? The answer is that while it may not hasten the onset of a stage, language may *consolidate* thinking at a given stage; it may make the child apply his thinking to a variety of different problems, all requiring operational thinking, but demanding the use of different combinations of elements. A thorough grounding in thinking at each stage is essential, for it is quite clear that the development of a subsequent stage is dependent on an adequate grounding in the previous stages.

Furthermore, it must be made quite clear that what we have been talking about has been the child's use of *his own* capacity for the production of language behaviour to aid thinking. While the relation between language and thinking in the child may not be developed fully until the stage of operational thinking, this obviously does not imply that *the teacher* should use language sparingly in his instruction of children at earlier stages of development. Such language behaviour by the teacher is important in two ways. Firstly, it can help the development of thinking; and secondly, it can help the child improve his language skills so that he can later use them as a tool to aid thinking.

6 THE TEACHER'S USE OF LANGUAGE TO ASSIST DEVELOPMENT OF THINKING

How, then, does the teacher use his own language behaviour to help the child's thinking? One obvious way is that he directs the child's *attention* to the important features of any situation. And he may not only draw attention to objects, but also to relations. The use of prepositions (see p. 47) is a prime example. He may employ this technique to varying degrees, perhaps using one word only to direct the child's attention to the key relation in a problem situation, then leaving him to solve the problem from there on. Further, the child's attention can be specifically directed to differences between objects, enabling him to distinguish between, for example, male and female sticklebacks. As a result of such a discrimination, he can not only distinguish his environment in more detail in respect to sticklebacks; having heard a label for the sex distinction, he may apply it elsewhere. Attention may not only be drawn to things present; the teacher might ask such questions as 'What will happen if you pour the water from this jug into this one?' By directing the child's attention to the future, the teacher is encouraging analysis of cause–effect. If the child's anticipation of what will happen is proved wrong by events, there is, furthermore, an ideal situation for accommodation.

The teacher's language behaviour does not only direct attention, however. It can also direct the child's *behaviour*. This is supremely obvious, but nevertheless worth stressing. For, given any situation, the child has several behavioural options open to him. Given some containers and some water, he can pour the water from one container to another; but there is a large number of possible alternative courses of action open to him. Indeed, this is why some teachers prefer not to employ activity methods – they cannot stand the uncertainty. The teacher can direct behaviour in advance by selecting the behavioural alternative for the child – pouring into other jugs (rather than christening other children). For it is a far more difficult task for the teacher to inhibit undesired behaviour once it has started than to initiate the desired behaviour at the beginning. And once again, as in the case of attention, teacher's utterances can refine behaviour; for example, by distinguishing verbally between reading out loud and reading to oneself, the teacher can direct the child into one of the two alternatives, perhaps making available to him a choice he did not have before.

Finally, the teacher's language behaviour can assist the child's thinking by acting as *feedback* during or after his performance of a task. This is what the teacher should be doing when he marks books. Part of the purpose of looking at children's work is to satisfy oneself that they have understood what one has taught; feedback to the teacher. But another part is feedback to the child; information from the teacher as to whether he is succeeding in whatever task he is doing. As age of pupil increases, so does the extent to which such feedback is provided for the child by the teacher marking his work after he has done it, and then returning it later. Yet this type of feedback appears to be far less efficient than the teacher telling the child how he is getting on while he is actually doing the task. For immediate feedback leads to the modification of the behaviour while it is still going on, whereas delayed feedback cannot do so. If the teacher goes round the class telling children where they are doing well and perhaps where they are going wrong, they are able to adapt their behaviour at any point in the sequence. But if they complete a piece of work and only learn later of their performance, they can only adapt if given a similar subsequent piece of work (by which time they have forgotten).

The teacher's immediate comments to the child may have other benefits besides improved feedback. First, they can act as signals for behaviour – he can not only tell him how he is doing but also suggest modification. Second, this may encourage the child to use his own language behaviour to regulate his performance. Third, the teacher's comments should act as reward; he is taking immediate interest in what she is doing. Behaviour followed closely by reward is more apt to recur than behaviour not so followed, so the teacher who goes round the class will take every opportunity of verbally praising the desired performance.

7 SUMMARY

A summary is required, since the present chapter is easily the most complex so far. We have suggested that the connection of language and thinking in the child requires certain previous events to have occurred. First, language has to have become internalized; that is, not only the language behaviour of others but also the child's own language has to regulate his behaviour. Secondly, thinking has to become operational, that is, as productive as language. It may be that language and thinking do not develop equally rapidly, so that language may have to wait for thinking to catch up before really productive inter-action can occur. However, this does not mean that the teacher should not use language freely to children of any age. For his use of language aids the child's thinking and language develop-ment, by regulating his attention and his behaviour, and by providing feedback.

7 Language and Personal Development

1 NATURE OF THE SELF-CONCEPT

Write your own entry in a new, revised, and democratic *Who's Who*, limiting yourself to twenty words. The result should be interesting to yourself, and even more interesting to your best friend! His interest is not surprising, for he is probably wondering whether you have seen yourself as others see you. Indeed, what you have written is intimately connected with others' views of you; for it is partly the behaviour of other people towards you which has formed the way you see yourself.

You have possibly included in your self-description indications of your *self-concept*; that is, your view of yourself as a person. You may see yourself as brighter than most, as attractive, as a socialist, etc. You may also have included clues as to the *social roles* you play – comedian, leader, shrinking violet, etc. A social role is a habitual pattern of behaviour in a social situation. The self-concept is intimately connected with one's development as a person, and will be discussed in the present chapter. A social role is a system regulating one's social skill, and will be dealt with in Chapter 8. However, the two are intimately connected; the girl who has attractiveness as part of her self-concept has probably derived that opinion of herself from the social role she plays at parties or in any mixed sex group; and the man who takes on the social role of leader of a group may do so because he has a concept of himself as an individual with leadership qualities.

It should be stressed here that in all probability we are not introducing processes which are different in kind from those described earlier. For the self-concept and the social role are probably names for particular sets of schemata in the brain functioning in a similar way to the schemata regulating language behaviour and other complex behaviour. Indeed, there are close parallels between the development of the self-concept and of morality on the one hand and the development of thinking on the other.

2 DEVELOPMENT OF THE SELF-CONCEPT

How does the self-concept *develop*? One source is imitation by the infant of someone else's behaviour, usually his mother's. At first he can only imitate immediately after the behaviour he is imitating has occurred. Soon, however, he can delay his imitation. What does such delayed imitation imply? It means that the child has *internalized* the behaviour of the other person as a model (see p. 53). He then regulates his own behaviour by this model, so that it approximates closer and closer to the model. This process is also known as *identification*, since the child identifies with the model, to whom he is attached by emotional bonds. The identification becomes less specific as the child becomes older; instead of imitating the actual behaviour or the mannerisms which it contains, the child imitates the attitudes of the model, the approval or disapproval of sorts of objects, events, or people. How then, it may be objected, can it happen that brothers and sisters, brought up in the same environment, develop very different self-concepts?

This leads us on to the other early source of the self-concept, the behaviour of others *towards the child himself*. Reward or punishment, praise or blame of the child are internalized by him. If he is punished and called a naughty boy, he will see himself as naughty. If he is told by teachers that he is poor at arithmetic, he will see himself as poor at it; and not realizing that others can be made to change their views of him, he may continue to see himself as poor.

As a result, then, of internalizing others' behaviour in general and their behaviour towards him in particular, the child comes to see himself as an actor, someone who does things; and he comes to see himself in comparison with others. Now, of course, this schema is changing continuously. It both *assimilates* evidence to itself and it *accommodates* itself to accord with the evidence. Suppose that the friends of the girl who considered herself attractive had had to write an entry in *Who's Who* for her. And suppose that they, as one woman, had considered her unattractive. What is she to do when shown their entries? (This, incidentally, is the best exercise for breaking up beautiful friendships that I know.) She could do one of two things. She could accommodate her self-concept to accord with the evidence, so that she considered herself smart rather than attractive. Or, she could assimilate the evidence to suit her self-concept. This would mean ignoring the evidence by adopting a defence mechanism against it, since it threatens her self-concept. She could, for example, rationalize the situation by supposing that they called her unattractive because they were jealous of her attractiveness. Some of us are excessively flexible in accommodating – we see ourselves as others see us so we have no consistent self-concept. Others are so inflexible that we see ourselves as someone totally different from the person others see us as; at the extreme, the schizophrenic may see himself as Napoleon.

So the self-concept, like other schemata, changes and adapts itself to new evidence. The child's self-concept, even though internalized, may be tied to *specific situations*. For example, he may see himself as a good boy at school but a bad boy at home. This will result from the different behaviour directed towards him in the two situations, which he had internalized; his mother may habitually scold him, while his teacher may praise him for his efforts. Another example: the child may see himself as a big boy in relation to his little brother and baby sister; for he has been treated by his mother and by them as big brother. However, on his arrival at the reception class, he finds himself one of the smallest boys in the school (and treated as such). So he may see himself as big, old, and important in the home setting but little, young, and insignificant at school.

3 THE SELF-CONCEPT IN ADOLESCENCE

The next step should be from a self-concept varying according to situation to one that is firstly, *self-consistent*, and secondly, *consistent over different situations*. However, few adolescents and not all adults apparently reach this stage of development. Why? One psychologist has called adolescence the crisis of identity. The adolescent has learned to look in on his self-concept – he has become conscious of it, and cannot make any sense out of it. He does not know who he is. Why not? One reason, of course, is that one would expect the self-concept to be *slower in developing* than thinking in general; for the self-concept is largely derived from approval or disapproval, reward or punishment at the hands of those to whom the child is attached. Therefore there is considerable anxiety associated with its establishment; anxiety concerning the threat of punishment or of withdrawal of affection. Such anxiety might well be expected to interfere with the development of a schema. Moreover, the self-concept has to be collated from many different sorts of experience, whereas other schemata may be derived from one area of experience.

A second reason for the disorganized nature of the self-concept in adolescence is the change of the *body-image* resulting from the growth spurt around puberty. The body-image is a source of stability in one's self-concept – at least one looks the same! Yet the changes at puberty are considerable; not only do adolescents grow bigger and change shape (within limits!). They do so at different ages, and girls reach puberty before boys. What is more, there are different attitudes towards the bodily changes and the sexual feelings that result. Some wish to conceal the fact that they are changing bodily and try to ignore the sexual feelings aroused. Others cannot wait to develop further, and engage in experimental sexual behaviour which horrifies some of their classmates. If the adolescent internalizes the behaviour and attitudes of others, which behaviour is he to internalize? And how will his self-concept adapt itself to the fact that while the majority of his group are looking, sounding, and behaving differently, he may as yet be a hairless soprano wolf-cub?

What is more, just at this time a number of *conflicting expectations* are made of him. He is expected to be adult in his social behaviour yet he is not allowed the money or the sexual freedom which he sees adults enjoy. He is expected to work as hard as an adult for deferred gratification when adults themselves obtain tangible rewards of status and pay for their labour. He is expected to obey his parents but not to demand their time and energy as he did when he was a child. He is treated as both child and adult, dependent and independent, irresponsible and responsible. It is little wonder that he finds difficulty in retaining any consistent form of self-concept.

His solution is often to obtain predictable behaviour from his age-group (*peer-group*). Their behaviour towards him can be internalized, so that he can derive his self-concept from the group he belongs to. The adolescent peer-group values solidarity, so the derivation of their self-concepts by its members from each other is unlikely to be disrupted. What is more, the peer-group values personality characteristics such as reticence, loyalty, and humour, so the member knows what is expected of him. The self-concept he derives from his peer-group in this way is totally different from that which he might derive from his school. For many schools value academic excellence, and therefore the self-concept derived from school is apt to be very limited in its scope. We might do well to treat the peer-group as a valuable source of experience and social learning rather than as an enemy. Perhaps, however, we do not see the development of the self-concept as one of the aims of education.

Even so, the adolescent is left with a self-concept derived largely from his membership of and relations within a group. He has yet to develop a self-concept which is consistent and *autonomous*. By autonomy is meant a condition where the person has integrated all of the following: the early identification with parent, the expectations of others in his group, and the traditional demands of society. He is dependent on none of these for his self-concept, but uses and transcends them all. He is an individual, continuously vigilant to preserve that individuality.

4 THE DEVELOPMENT OF ATTITUDES AND MORALITY

The sequence of the development of the self-concept, then, is one of internalization. Behaviour is imitated, internalized, and then what is internalized is organized. Closely related to it is the development of *morality and attitudes*. Attitudes are schemata which regulate evaluative behaviour, approval or disapproval, towards things or events or actions or people. They have the same source as the self-concept – the imitation of the model. In this case, they are derived from the evaluative behaviour of the model towards people other than the child or actions other than his. The child first imitates such behaviour, then internalizes it, making his own the attitudes which regulate it in others. Thus the only difference between the child's self-concept and attitudes is that the former is mainly derived from the model's behaviour towards the child himself, the latter from the model's behaviour towards others.

Obviously, it is particularly important with whom the child identifies in the case of attitudes. If he is a boy, he is likely to identify with his father, and perhaps internalize the more masculine attitudes of our society, aggressive ambition and dominance. Incidentally, morals are defined in this chapter as that sub-section of attitudes which are considered particularly important by our society; these are primarily attitudes concerning other people, property, and institutions.

How do attitudes change and *develop*? By progressive assimilation and accommodation, like any other schemata. What has been internalized gradually becomes consistent and systematized. In the earlier stage of development, attitudes are limited in precisely the same way as are other schemata. For example, a child at the pre-operational stage (see p. 55) cannot take both intention and results into account; he will say that the child who broke twelve cups while trying to help is worse than the child who broke one cup while trying to steal the jam. This is obviously similar to inability to conserve – allowing the length of, for example, a lump of Plasticine to dominate judgements of its size.

Later accommodation and assimilation is more difficult. For attitudes are generally favourable or unfavourable constructions we put on *general* classes of events or people, so it usually takes more than one piece of contrary evidence to make them accommodate. Children may have learned unfavourable attitudes to black people from parents; so a contrary piece of evidence consisting of the friendly behaviour of a black child at school may be easily avoided: the black child may be 'the exception that proves the rule', or they may be 'different when they're children'. It is very easy to rationalize away a piece of contrary evidence to an attitude.

Another example, to show on the other hand how attitudes may accommodate to evidence. The child may have been taught a negative attitude to smoking, yet he sees his teacher, whom he admires, smoking. How is he to accommodate his attitudes? One way is to modify his attitudes both to teacher and to smoking, to bring them closer together. The teacher is not quite so admirable, and smoking is not quite so bad. Another way is to discover another virtue in the teacher which pushes the child's estimation of him back up to the former level. This example is of interest because it shows how *suggestion* works – the child's attitude to smoking might have been modified because it was associated with someone he admired. Irrational, but it happens!

Once again, as in the case of language and thinking, the final stage in development of attitudes is a self-consistent body of attitudes which can be *productive*. In other words, one can create and envisage new moral codes or sets of values. One can, as it were, step outside one's attitudes and values and manipulate them to see what the result will be. All systems which reverse the currently held set of values are the results of such manipulations; the creeds of hippies, student revolutionaries, and Enoch Powell, are present-day examples, those of Socrates and Christ historical ones. So productivity is a feature of the final stage of development of attitudes as well as of thinking and language.

5 LANGUAGE AND THE EARLY DEVELOPMENT OF THE SELF-CONCEPT AND ATTITUDES

A lot of space has been devoted to describing personal development without mentioning the part language plays. I felt this was necessary because the psychology of personal and social development contains many concepts with which you may be unfamiliar. This is in marked contrast to Chapter 3, where I assumed I did not need to define subject and predicate, noun and verb. Why? Perhaps because the schools in which we were educated did not consider knowledge of personal development as important as knowledge of the structure of language. Is this priority correct?

What part does language play in personal development? Psychologists have not yet explored the field to any extent, but we can make a few informed guesses. Consider the earliest stage of development of the self-concept. The child imitates and internalizes others' behaviour in general and their behaviour towards him in particular. One aspect of the adult's general behaviour the child imitates is what the adult says. As we noted in Chapter 4, the imitation is not perfect. The child does not say the same sentences as the adult, but the basic sense is the same. Mummy may say to herself 'I think I'll do the washing up now', and the child may imitate, some time later, 'Do washing up now.' The mother has been using language to plan her behaviour, and the child has imitated. He has internalized language which implies acting on the environment; later he, too, may use it to regulate his behaviour. The point is that such imitation permits the child to see himself as potential actor on and changer of his environment.

Consider, too, the case where the child imitates and internalizes the language used to him by his mother. She may call him a naughty boy or a good boy in different situations. She will certainly address him by his name, as a result of which he will see himself as an individual, separate from others. More subtly, the *function* of her utterances may affect his self-concept; if she is continuously prohibiting or commanding, he may see himself as one who is not a chooser but an obeyer; if she asks him questions, he may see himself as an instructor, a source of information.

The same applies to the development of *attitudes*. The mother or father may express an attitude of approval or disapproval about anyone or anything. Their attitude may come across by the tone of voice as much as by the actual sense. All the child has to understand to be able to internalize such attitudes is who or what his parent are talking about. Value words such as good, bad, nice, nasty, clean, dirty also may play a big part in this process; they may at first only be understood when they are accompanied by appropriate adult behaviour.

Since the child at school may identify with the teacher, there is a considerable possibility that the child may internalize his attitudes, both spoken and acted out. Which attitudes should he make public to his pupils?

6 LANGUAGE AND THE SYSTEMATIZATION OF THE SELF-CONCEPT AND ATTITUDES

It is perhaps, in the *organization of the self-concept* that language is most important. Once internalization has occurred, the child's task is to make his self-concept more consistent internally and over different situations. This stage is where his own language behaviour, both uttered and internalized is vital. For he is now at the operational stage of thinking where *his own* language can affect the organization of his self-concept.

To what extent do the older primary school child and the adolescent make use of language to describe themselves? Probably very little in a direct way. But in fact they are very often talking about themselves indirectly when apparently they are talking about something or someone else. They may identify themselves with someone who represents their ideal self-concept, the person they think they could be, given half a chance. Or they may criticize a friend for displaying characteristics which either they don't like in themselves, or, more subtly, which they would like to display but dare not.

The adolescent's language behaviour describing himself directly or indirectly may be modified and made more consistent by asking questions which gradually change the reference from other people to the adolescent himself. For example, questions about which pop star the adolescent would like to be can be narrowed down to questions about what he would do if he were that pop star; then the question arises as to why he would behave in this way. Inconsistencies in the adolescent's self-concept will rapidly appear; he will, for example, say that he would be popular, a show man and a one for the girls, but at the same time a homelover and a family lover, avoiding publicity. These inconsistencies in what he says may well strike him; if they don't, a comment or question will make them obvious.

The example quoted may well be useful in inducing consistency in another sense; it might help to bridge the gap between the adolescent's *ideal* self and his *real* self. It might in other words, make his self-concept more realistic; more realistic in the sense that it accords more with his actual abilities and circumstances. If the adolescent can describe himself as he sees himself, and contrast this with the sort of person he would like to be, then at least he has made the gap between the reality and his ideal more explicit and obvious to himself. This may result in the modification of his ideal to approximate to a realistic self-concept; or in the modification of his self-concept to approximate more closely to his ideal.

I have been suggesting, then, that talking aloud about his idea of himself is a useful factor in aiding the adolescent's development of a systematic self-concept. It is useful because the language behaviour he may be led to use about himself may be internalized and affect his self-concept. The same applies to expression of *attitudes*. If the adolescent is asked for his attitudes, he may be made to express verbally favourable or unfavourable attitudes of which he was not fully aware. This parallels the case of the self-concept – the child may not be aware that when he is talking about other people he may in fact be talking about himself. The first benefit which arises, then, from verbal expression of attitudes is that the adolescent is made more aware of them.

The second benefit is that, as in the case of the self-concept, this verbal expression may be *modified* by someone else. The adult may ask what the adolescent's opinion on the abuse of drugs is and then ask his opinion of the abuse of alcohol. The adolescent may notice an inconsistency in his own statements; or the adult may ask if they are different cases, and why, thus bringing any self-contradiction out into the open. We are back with our familar processes of accommodation and assimilation; in this case, the evidence is the person's own words.

It is worth noting that the point about accommodation that

F

was made in Chapter 1 is applicable here too; if the evidence is *too* contrary to the existing schema, accommodation will not take place. So in this case, if the adult utters *his* attitudes, which may well be in complete opposition to those of the adolescent, the adolescent is unlikely to accommodate to them. In the same way, if the adult had given his opinion of the character of the adolescent would-be pop star, this would have diverged so much from the adolescent's self-concept that no accommodation would have occurred. The conclusion must be that the adult's task in such a situation is to elicit attitudes from others, not to utter his own.

Many of us find this a terribly hard task, particularly when we feel that our own attitudes are right. Most tempting is the use of suggestion (see p. 68) to change attitudes, especially if we know we are popular. Since suggestion is a non-rational procedure, both (*a*) confrontation of our own with pupils' attitudes and (*b*) confrontation of pupil's attitudes with their own inconsistencies are preferable to it. For the basic point of attitude training is to induce rational consideration of attitudes rather than suggestion. Of the two alternatives, the writer prefers (*b*), on the grounds that both the attitudes of the pupil are already internalized, and therefore intolerance of inconsistency is more likely.

In summary, it has been shown that the development of the self-concept and of attitudes follows the same principle of internalization as language and thinking. The difficulties of forming a consistent self-concept and set of attitudes during adolescence were stressed. The language behaviour of others was shown to play an important part in the internalization process, while the language behaviour of the adolescent himself was shown to affect the systematization process.

8 Language and Social Development

I THE DEVELOPMENT OF SOCIAL ROLES

The very earliest experiences of a child's life are social. Indeed, he is born with certain reflex behaviours designed to promote social contact with his mother. Smiling, crying, sucking, clinging, and following with the eyes all lead to attention to the child by the mother. By six or seven months the child can recognize his mother as different from others. So from the earliest period of his life, the child is learning to interact with other people.

The development of *social roles* in the child follows the same process of *internalization* which we have seen in the development of the self-concept. The child observes how others behave in groups, how they interact. He sees how smaller children behave when they are with bigger children; how passengers behave on a bus; how children play games with rules, like tag or hopscotch. He later internalizes this evidence, and forms regular patterns of his own behaviour in given types of situation. Obviously, such expectations depend on the existence of a self-concept, since he has to see himself as an agent who can act on other people.

Having internalized his experience of groups of people, and having acquired several different roles to suit different sorts of situation, how does the child refine and develop his role-playing behaviour? How does he learn the way to control his high opinion of himself when he is with older children, or to control his aggression when he is frustrated in his aims by authority? How does he improve the way he eats in company, asks the way of strangers, introduces himself to people, or takes a joke?

Once again, the process is one of *assimilation and accommodation*. In this case, the evidence is the effect his behaviour has on other people. The evidence, in other words, is the *feedback* from his own behaviour. He may assimilate the evidence to suit a role that turns out to be false. For example, he may see himself as leader of a group, but find that when he makes a suggestion as to what to do next, nobody takes him up on it. He may assimilate this evidence by rationalizing that they do not appreciate the point of his suggestion because they are too stupid. Or he may accommodate to it, and change his role to another, not that of leader, in that particular situation. From this example it is obvious that the child has to be very flexible in changing his roles to suit the situation. Imaginative play is a big help to the child trying to acquire this flexibility, for he can pretend to be, for example, a daddy, and see what sort of behaviour is acceptable to his 'wife' and 'children'.

2 THE DEVELOPED SKILLS OF ROLE-PLAYING

What, then, are these skills which a person with developed social roles requires? The first has already been mentioned – the skill of choosing the role *to suit* the occasion. The role of class joker may be more appropriate for the child outside the classroom than inside it when the teacher is explaining something to the class.

The second is the related ability to *switch* roles when the situation changes. The student teacher, for example, has to switch roles from being a learner, sitting at the back and watching when the regular teacher is still in the room, but taking the role of teacher when he is on his own. The same conflict of roles occurs when he has to teach in front of his supervisor. Children, too, have to adapt to changes in the social situation. A new teacher may play a different role to the previous teacher, so children have to change their roles too; the new teacher may play an authority role, demanding obedience, while the previous one may have played an advisory role, offering suggestions; so the boy who rejected suggestions previously will find himself suffering for disobeying commands now, unless he adapts his role.

In such a situation, both sides will put efforts into *defining* their new role; the new teacher will ensure that the pupils perceive the role he is playing. He will do so by stressing those features of his own and his pupils' behaviour which concern his exercise of authority and their reactions to him. He may come down hard on relatively minor 'offences' in order to show from the start that *he* is in charge. The pupils too, of course, may define their own roles, either subservient or rebellious. They too, will behave in such a way as to make it quite clear to the teacher which role they are adopting.

Another skill that comes with good role-playing is that the child can use his role-playing to *change systems*. He can, for example, cast himself for long enough as the bully to persuade the teacher to change the seating arrangements in the class or he may ask or answer questions so stupidly as to disrupt a teaching programme completely. A final mature skill is the ability to *maintain* a role, where necessary, for a long period of time. Teachers have to learn to play whatever role they have chosen for themselves for as long as they are in the classroom. If they break the role, if they suddenly become confidant instead of consultant, or one of the boys instead of one of the teachers, embarrassment results; for the pupils because their expectations of how a teacher should behave are confounded, and for the teacher because, for example, he will have to listen to the children's criticism of his colleagues. It is evident, then, that to be skilled in social behaviour, a person has to have many roles available to him, and he has to be able to choose the appropriate one.

By this time, you will be objecting that social behaviour has been cynically made to appear a mere act. People do not change chameleon-like to every changing circumstance, they are not all things to all men. Agreed: roles are not the only schemata people use. Their self-concept limits the number of roles available, and ensures some consistency. Someone who sees himself as left-wing and radical is likely to avoid old boy rugger clubs where he may have to play a role inconsistent with his self-concept. Children who see themselves as academic failures will opt out of any situation where they have to play the role of academic learners, and, probably, academic losers. They choose many alternative roles, and make themselves very skilled at performing them. In school they may be class joker, rebel, or outsider. But these are often not rewarding enough, so they acquire a role in a peer-group. One final point – to what extent does practice in the academic winner role or the other less approved roles which schools require prepare children for some of the roles needed in adult life? Father, mother, employee, union member, interviewee, breadwinner, husband, wife, juryman, foreman . . . ?

3 LANGUAGE AND THE DEVELOPMENT OF SOCIAL ROLES

The young child observes others' behaviour in social situations and imitates it. One clue that he gets about what is going on in a group situation is the *language behaviour* of the members of that group. He will hear one member telling another what to do and criticizing him for not doing it correctly. Or he may hear one child comparing himself with another, saying that he is bigger, older or better. Or he may hear a child trying to make peace or to comfort another. In other words, the child at this stage uses the language behaviour in the group to help him *distinguish* the roles that the members of the group are playing.

Having distinguished the different roles, he may then *select* one for internalization. Such selection might depend on his self-concept; he might not see himself as being capable of being a leader and so choose not to imitate a leader; or a girl might have identified strongly with her mother's loving care, and as a result might imitate the child who was the group's peacemaker and comforter. The point is that the language behaviour of the group allows the child to distinguish the different roles being played and thus to have alternatives from which to select.

When the child has internalized a few roles, he has to try them out. He now has to use language behaviour as a *social tool* for use rather than as a clue for observation. If he sets himself up as leader of a group, he has to be in full mastery of the imperative grammatical construction! He has to issue his commands, and utter some threats to ensure obedience. He has to make plans for future action and dismiss alternative proposals. If, on the other hand, he tries out the role of group funny man, he has to possess different linguistic skills – the ability to parody others' speech and perhaps to make outrageous puns.

Not only does he have to use these linguistic tools himself; he also has to understand the linguistic response of other group members to his utterances. If his arguments in favour of his plan of action are rejected, he has to understand why they were rejected. He has to use the rejection, in other words, as *feedback* so that he can adapt his language behaviour next time. Such experience refines his use of language as a tool in the exercise of his social role.

This sort of feedback is particularly available in *play* situations. For in imaginative play it does not matter so much if the child is clumsy in his efforts to play a role. He can use language imaginatively in his efforts to find out how far he can go as a daddy, a teacher, a bus conductor. He can even make silly mistakes on purpose, to assure himself that they are mistakes. For example, when pretending to be a teacher, he can ask a 'pupil', 'Please can I go to the toilet?' He gets a laugh by this question, thus assuring himself that the teacher's role involves giving permission, the pupil's asking it.

4 LANGUAGE AND THE DEVELOPED SKILLS OF ROLE-PLAYING

Language behaviour needs to be employed even more finely as a tool if the advanced skills described in Section 2 of this chapter are to be developed. The first skill mentioned there was *suiting the role* to fit the situation. Choosing a role in a hurry involves having available simultaneously several roles to choose from. And having several roles available also means having several varieties of language behaviour simultaneously available: One adolescent may be leader of his own peer-group but junior in a group of boys older than himself. He has to have available a set of dominating and a set of submissive language behaviours. He has to be able to distinguish them, so that he can select the right one for the right occasion; and he has to be able to switch from one to the other if one situation changes to the other.

It is worth stressing that such a switch does not just involve a change of tone. He will have to talk less when he is with the older boys, ask questions or make tentative suggestions rather than utter commands, and give way when he happens to start talking at the same time as another boy.

The converse of ability to switch roles is the ability to *maintain* a role for a long period where necessary. Here the difficulty is to keep to the language behaviour required by the role; one must not allow items from language behaviour suited to other roles to creep in. Difficulties otherwise result. The teacher who swears has allowed behaviour relevant to another role to creep in to his role as classroom teacher. The working-class boy who calls the master 'mate' has made a similar mistake. Both mistakes are possibly unintentional – the teacher or the pupil did not wish to use language to create another role for themselves (unless, that is, the teacher was trying to be one of the boys). But the extent to which language is a vital tool to maintain a role is evident from the way roles break down when such linguistic mistakes occur.

The extent to which different language *registers* (that is, types of language behaviour suited to different roles) are used by pupils often upsets adults. They hear adolescents talking to each other in a mid-Atlantic drawl and using the words of the beat and hippy sub-cultures; and they shudder. The point is that they are using different language registers to fit different roles. Since the roles are very different, so are the registers. It is fortunate that adolescents do learn different registers to suit their roles at home, at school, and with their peers; and it is important that they should select the right register to fit the right role. Teachers should aim to encourage language behaviour suited to the classroom situation. The reason why alternative registers and correct selection are important is evident from the roles the pupil will have to play in adult life. Suppose the pupil becomes a teacher in adult life. The registers appropriate to teacher, to husband and to father differ very considerably. Failure to select the correct register can be fatal to the role concerned – especially if he uses the teacher register in the husband role!

5 IMPLICATIONS FOR TEACHING

What implications do the connections between language behaviour and social role have for the teacher? Firstly, consider the classroom situation. There are different roles being played by teacher and by pupils. Teacher may be instructor one minute, disciplinarian the next, and peacemaker the next. She may vary her role depending on whether she is addressing the class as a whole, small groups, or individuals. Pupils, too, may vary roles dependent on situation. Language behaviour is therefore very important, because it gives clues to others as to which role one is playing at that moment, and therefore as to how they ought to react.

Perhaps changing language behaviour to suit changing role is one of the most difficult things a *teacher* has to learn. It is also one of the most vital to acquire, because if pupils do not know which role a teacher is playing at any given moment, they do not know the appropriate role to play themselves. Some teachers are considered two-faced by their pupils because, ironically, there is not a clear enough distinction between their two faces! The teacher may appear to the children to be humorous when in fact he is being sarcastic and punitive. He has not made it clear which role he is playing, so the children react to the wrong role, and probably suffer for it. Of course, teachers are many-faced; they have to be, but they must make it clear which face they are wearing.

If this skill is so important, how does it function and how may the training teacher acquire it? There are many people who can modify on demand their tone of voice and its volume, and also their facial expression and often gestures. They are often extraverts, who enjoy making an impression on people, and need to do so to keep their self-esteem. But it does not 'come naturally' to many others. Perhaps one way of acquiring it is to act out roles to fellow students, and have them guess which out of several roles one is playing. Also, it would be valuable to have them criticize one's performance, as there is always the danger of overplaying. A tape recorder is an obvious accessory, closed circuit television a luxurious one.

The use of the correct language for different roles is necessary for teachers. It is also necessary for *pupils*. It seems that in many schools the only language register they acquire at school is that of learner. However, it would surely be beneficial to acquire suitable language for other roles, for example, parent, employee, husband or wife. Such skills would not only be useful to the pupil when he leaves school and gets married. They could also help his social awareness while still at school.

For one way of teaching the appropriate language register to a role which they do not at present have to play is to make pupils *play the role* themselves. They can be interviewer for a job, parent correcting child, shop-steward addressing a meeting, or even teacher instructing a class. Having to play a role means that one has to represent to oneself the behaviour appropriate to it. And having to represent the role to himself means that the operationally thinking child can compare different roles representationally. The language register of each role will assist such comparisons. For example, the pupil will have to act as parent correcting a child. He finds he has to use a reproving and yet a reasoning tone. He may compare his representation of this role with his own reactions to correction. Such a comparison might lead to a greater understanding of the roles others play, and therefore a modification of his own roles in response. In other words the child might acquire empathy, the skill of putting oneself in another's shoes. And then might come sympathy, the ability to play the appropriate role in response to the role you have perceived the other to be playing.

6 SUMMARY

In summary, we have seen in this chapter that the *development* of social roles is similar to the development of thinking and of the self-concept and attitudes in that it has to be *internalized* from outside evidence. The evidence in this case is the behaviour other people use when they are in groups. The *use* of social roles is a very complex skill; one has to select a role to suit a situation, switch roles to suit changes in situation, and maintain a role over a lengthy period of time.

Language is of importance both in the development and in the playing of social roles. In development, the language of others in a social situation helps the child to distinguish the roles that are being played. When actually engaging in a role he employs his own language as a tool to further his social aims; and he uses the language behaviour of others as feedback information about how succesfully he is playing his role. He has to have simultaneously at his disposal several registers of language behaviour to suit the different roles he may be called upon to play. Role-playing by pupils and by student teachers acting a role they do not at present play was suggested as a means of developing such social skills.

9 Language Behaviour in the Classroom

I COMMUNICATION

What goes on in classrooms? Nobody knows except the children and the teacher. Other teachers do not know, since they only have the evidence of what their colleague chooses to tell them; and this may be coloured by his desire to impress or his fear of criticism. Student teachers do not know, since it seems quite likely that the class teacher will put on a special show for them. Head teachers do not know, since they are too busy administrating, or because a special show will be put on for them too. Research workers do not know, since their very presence and activity changes the social situation of the classroom completely. So all we can do is make informed guesses.

Consider again the examples of *communication* we cited in Chapter 1. In the case of the lecture, the sender of the message was the lecturer, and the receivers were his audience of students. He received no verbal feedback as to whether the students were understanding what he was saying, but he may have received some visual feedback concerning how bored they were and whether they were paying attention or not. This may well be true with some teachers. They spend almost all their time talking to the class. Periodically they ask questions, but these questions are often aimed at providing feedback concerning the class's attention. They might even ask for a repetition from a pupil of what they have just said. Sometimes, their questions are aimed at discovering whether the class has understood what they have explained. In this case, there is one correct answer which they expect; other answers are wrong.

Other teachers communicate in a similar way to the couple deciding what to do for the evening. That is, both teacher and pupils are senders and receivers of messages. Both can modify what they say next as a result of hearing what the other has just said. This is, of course true of the 'lecturer'. But in his case, the change he makes in what he says is not likely to be a change of content. Suppose he discovers that a child gives the wrong answer; if he is conscientious he will explain again the point which has been misunderstood, perhaps by rephrasing his explanation. If he is not, he will feed the correct answer to the pupil in order to obtain it and satisfy himself that his explanation is clear. In the case of the 'conversationalist' type of teacher, however, the pupils' messages to him may result in his changing the content of his own messages as he goes along.

Choice of communication technique obviously depends on teacher's *aims*. If he wishes to present a carefully programmed piece of instruction he will choose the 'lecturer' type of communication. If he wishes to accept relevant and irrelevant examples of the point under discussion, he will choose the 'conversationalist' technique. The advantage of the latter technique is that it involves the children and their interests and experience; its disadvantage is the difficulty of keeping to the subject. Of course, it is idealistic to suppose that all teachers vary techniques to suit their purpose; it is more likely that many employ the technique which fits their personality.

The previous discussion, however, assumes that communication is the only event occurring in the classroom. In junior schools, this is highly unlikely. Usually, communication between teacher and pupil occurs in the context of a *task* on which the child is engaged. The purpose of language behaviour to communicate is thus inextricably linked in these situations with its purpose in regulating behaviour. Suppose the child is engaged in arranging a row of cubes in order of size. He might send the first message, 'Please, Miss, I can't find where this one goes.' The reply might be 'Try putting it there', in which case the teacher's reply has regulated his behaviour. Or it might be 'Put each brick in between the next bigger and the next smaller one', in which case the child might repeat this instruction to himself, using it as a rule to regulate his subsequent behaviour.

It is quite clear that in the case where language is fulfilling both its basic functions of communication and regulation, then the 'conversationalist' technique is more appropriate. The children will probably be employed on different tasks, so the teacher will not be communicating with the whole class. And apart from questioning the teacher's initial explanation of what he has to do, the child is only apt to communicate when his own regulation of his behaviour in the task has proved inadequate. Of course, this does not imply that the teacher cannot initiate communication; he might provide a new verbal rule which will enable the child to do a lot more with the task material than he had done so far. But it does mean that communication, when it occurs, is going to be two-way, and that it is going to be concerned with the regulation of behaviour.

Finally, and very important indeed, communication by means of language behaviour is a necessary social skill, and children who are only receivers of messages are only learning part of this skill; they must learn to send messages as well. The importance of taking the receiver into account when formulating a message is paramount (see Chapter 1). So is the importance of suiting the message to the occasion (see Chapter 8).

2 REGULATION

It was stressed in Chapter 6 that the regulation of other behaviour by means of language behaviour requires *internalization* of language. It was stated that the development of internalization is in three stages. The first is that the child's behaviour is regulated by his mother's language behaviour; the second, that he tells himself aloud what to do; the third, that the system which regulated his language behaviour comes to regulate his other behaviour too.

The second stage is very important, since it is a necessary intermediary between the first and the third. Yet it may not be encouraged in the classroom. Some teachers are afraid that children threaten their authority by talking at all; others are very willing for children to talk to them, the teachers, but not to each other or to themselves. Yet these last two examples of language behaviour represent the second stage of internalization; the child is either telling his group or himself what to do. He needs the prop of language behaviour to enable him to perform the task (unless the task is a routine, overlearned piece of behaviour). For language has the flexibility which allows different permutations of language items and therefore different arrangements of materials to be made.

It is also extremely important for *older* pupils to make explicit the principles they are using to solve a problem. If internalized language is helping to regulate their behaviour, it is often beneficial to externalize it. Then the principles they are using can be made clear to themselves and to the teacher, or possible new principles may become evident. The difficulty of working-class children in externalizing their internalized language in this way has already been described in Chapter 5. It is evident that this difficulty will diminish the teacher's estimate of their ability and also perhaps leave them unclear as to the principles involved.

It was made clear in Chapter 7 that one's *self-concept* resulted partly from the internalization of the language behaviour of others used to and about oneself. Therefore the expression, or externalization, of this internalized language will lead to awareness of the nature of the self-concept by the self and by others. A curriculum based on academic subjects allows little of this externalization to occur. The sort of classroom situation in which it can occur is usually of an informal and imaginative nature. For, as was remarked earlier, adolescents are unlikely to talk about themselves. Therefore, they can best be assisted to an awareness of their self-concept by means of situations into which they project themselves. They are talking about themselves without realizing it when they are describing or acting out their ambitions and interests. The realization that they are so doing may then be gradually induced by skilful comment.

Social roles, too, depend on the internalization and adoption of the language behaviour of others in groups (see Chapter 8). The number of social roles the child has available may be a function of the number of different language registers of which he is master. Here, too, the exercise and externalization of these language registers is important. For it makes clear to the child that he has available the tool to play a particular social role which he did not think was open to him before. Of course, any form of group work permits the exercise of social roles. But how often does the teacher encourage a child to use the language register of a role he seldom plays? And how often does the child play a role which is not in practice open to him yet (e.g. mummy, teacher)?

This section, then, is a plea for *expression*; firstly, because expression makes clear to the pupil some of the principles by which he is regulating his behaviour; secondly, because it tells the teacher about the pupil's understanding and personality; and thirdly, because the teacher can modify the expressed language behaviour. There is, then, the chance that the pupil will re-internalize this modified version.

An example of this last point will close the section and raise a fundamental *moral question*. The teacher may have succeeded in eliciting from a boy the claim that he sees himself as a hard man, caring for no authority and safe from its constraints because of the strength and solidarity of his friends. The teacher may also have got the boy to admit that there might well be cases where authority could catch up with him. If, for example, he killed a pedestrian by the reckless or drunken driving of his motor-cycle, he would be arrested. The boy might modify his self-concept as a result. We would all probably agree that this was desirable.

Yet the moral question raised is clear. To what extent is the teacher justified in modifying the self-concept by verbal or any other means? The teacher takes it for granted that he is justified in modifying the intellectual development of the child. He has the curriculum (particularly in the secondary school) to bolster his confidence that he is modifying it in the right direction. But what of social and personal development? The teacher is affecting the child's personal and social development, whether he explicitly intends to or not, simply by being his teacher. Perhaps what is most important is that he should be *aware* of his own self-concept, attitudes and roles, and of the ways in which these will affect his pupils.

3 LANGUAGE AND SKILLED READING

If little is known about what goes on in classrooms (see Section 1), even less is known about the development of *reading*. Much research has been carried out on the superiority of method X over method Y, but most teachers say that children seem to learn by whatever method they are taught. The reason for this is that reading is not a separate skill, to be taught by particular methods. Rather, it is an aspect of language behaviour. Therefore differences in reading ability may be due to differences in linguistic skill; and the universal possession of a certain degree of linguistic skill may ensure that children conscientiously taught by any accepted method learn to read in the end.

In what ways is reading similar to other language behaviour, and what ways is it different? It is *similar*, firstly, in its basic purpose – *communication*. The reader's object is to understand the message. Secondly, it is similar in that involves the same series of *sub-skills* (see Chapter 3), phonological, grammatical, and semantic. Thirdly, it is similar in that there are contextual *constraints* operating within each sub-skill and between sub-skills.

Let me elaborate this last point further. The words 'drate' and 'skice' sound as though they might be invented by the washing-powder manufacturers, whereas 'pshoop' and 'srate' definitely do not. Why? Because there are *constraints* operating as to which speech sounds can occur together at the beginning of a word; dr and sk are permissible, psh and sr are not. Similarly, in terms of grammar, one can say, 'the big red ball', but not 'ball big the red'; even 'the red big ball' is unlikely. Semantic constraints ensure that one cannot say 'The table laughed', or 'Pass me some typewriter' (although one can say 'Pour me some tea'). And all constraints from each sub-skill act upon each other; for example, consider the sentences, 'The subject of our discussion today is the learning of reading' and 'Don't subject me to such boredom'. The 'sub' of 'subject' is stressed in the first case but not in the second. On its own, this phonological distinction might be hard to spot, but with the grammatical constraints of the auxiliary verbs 'don't' and the direct object 'me', and with the overall semantic constraints, it is difficult to make a mistake.

The aspect of language behaviour that we call reading is subject to exactly the same constraints as other language

G

behaviour. The skilled reader, like the skilled listener, uses all the clues he can get from what he has just read to help him with the next bit. In fact, just like the skilled listener, he constructs what is going to occur before it actually does so. Just as the skilled listener can tell you what you are going to say next if you pause in mid-sentence, so the skilled reader will anticipate what is going to be written later on in the line. This is why he only focuses his eyes on a few points in a line of print. It is not so much that he can see all the rest out of the corner of his eye; rather, he has constructed what he has missed out, and is focusing on one or two points to ensure that his guesses are correct. So he does not focus on function words such as 'the', so much as on the basic subject of the sentence, the actor, or the verb, the action, or the object, who or what that action is done to.

For the skilled reader, then, reading a book involves the same language skills as understanding a speaker. What are the basic *differences* between these two processes? The first is the very obvious one that the reader is using *visual* cues, the listener *auditory* ones. Because of the nature of visual cues, spatial skill is involved in using them. Auditory cues occur in time, however, and so sequencing skills are particularly involved in their case. For the skilled reader, this makes little difference. He has mastered the different shapes of groups of letters, the fact that they occur in left-to-right, top-to-bottom order and all the other spatial skills involved. The only advantage of a written message is that he can go back to the beginning of a sentence again if he has forgotton it by the time he reaches the end! The listener has to interrupt the speaker and ask him to repeat what he has just said. Writers usually make the most of this advantage by inflicting long and complex sentences on their readers!

4 LANGUAGE AND LEARNING TO READ

But what is the difference between reading a book and understanding a speaker for the child who is about to learn to read? The most obvious point is that he has to graft a new language sub-skill on to an already well-established one. He has to graft the spatial skills of reading on to the phonological skills of speech perception and production. But the basic phonological skills are by now automatic, and the grammatical and semantic skills are fairly well developed. So the difficulty is that of developing a new and difficult addition to an already familiar and well-mastered set of skills; the spatial skills have to be brought up to the level of the familiar language skills before reading becomes as fluent as understanding speech.

Methods of development of *spatial skills* involved have been the subject of argument. Either one says that they have to be mastered by themselves before other language sub-skills can be brought to bear on reading; or one says that all the other sub-skills should be used to assist the acquisition of the new spatial skill. The writer supports the latter approach, since it seems a waste of potential not to use all the resources available.

It should be noted that most methods of teaching reading that have been used have adopted the former approach, that of developing spatial skills in isolation. This is more obvious in the case of *phonic* methods, where letters or letter strings are linked with speech sounds. This is often not linking the spatial cues even with phonological skill, since phonological skill involves the *combination* of speech sounds. Recent research shows that children who are successfully learning to read recognize not isolated letters representing isolated sounds but strings of letters representing combinations of sounds. In particular, they recognize those which form small function words, such as 'the', or inflexions, such as '–ing', '–ly'. Also, they recognize those clusters which are lawful in certain positions e.g. 'dr' as opposed to 'sr' at the beginning of a word. This indicates that their phonological skills affect their recognition of written language behaviour even though they may have been taught individual letter shapes.

It is also clear that *look and say* whole word methods do not make use of phonological, grammatical, or semantic skills. Look and say forces the child to distinguish shapes of printed words by showing him individual printed words and in some cases an accompanying picture; the shapes concerned are those of individual words, not letters or letter strings. It is supposed that this method is effective, partly because it allows the child to perceive a meaning. The meaning is supposed to be the connection between the individual single word and the 'thing' to which it refers. But in fact the method is based on the fallacy that a word has a meaning. Words are not the units of meaning; meaning involves the understanding of a message, and few messages consist of one word. When they do, it is only because the sender is confident that the receiver will construct the intended sentence round the word. Look and say methods, then, do not use grammatical or semantic skills, since they do not involve the combination of words in sentences from the start; they ignore phonological skill, since they do not associate letter strings with combinations of sounds.

Which methods, then, will ensure use of established language skills in learning to read? All possible cues ought to be highlighted in the teaching situation. As was shown in Chapter 4, *the non-linguistic context* of utterance gives important cues for understanding an utterance. Let the context of utterance be present for written language too. The sentence might be 'The train's going towards the tunnel'. Let there be a toy train and a tunnel, let them be arranged with the train to the left and the tunnel to the right, and make the train go towards the tunnel. Language behaviour is used to communicate – why should written language not describe a present state of affairs? Most of the child's spoken language at this age will concern his immediate environment. So the use of non-linguistic context will encourage the use of language skill as a whole.

Semantic cues are also applicable. Overall semantic content might be supplied from the start by reading to the child aloud the short story which he will shortly have to read. Specific semantic cues could be highlighted by means of the non-linguistic context again. For example, in the sentence quoted, the toy train should first be shown stationary behind the written phrase 'The train'. The child's semantic skill will lead to his supplying the word 'go' in some form, since he has mastered the semantic rule that allows movement words to be used of modes of transport. The child may then move the train towards the tunnel himself, in which case the teacher can follow the train's progress along the track with his finger along the written sentence. With prompting, the child will say 'The train's going towards the tunnel', and so will himself have supplied the sentence to be read.

Grammatical clues may be highlighted by visual means, within the written sentence. Subject and predicate (the major distinction) might be on different levels of print. They are the most important grammatical units because they tell the child what is being talked about and what is being said about it. Grammar and understanding are as closely related to each other as are semantics and understanding. Lower-level grammatical clues, such as the fact that article and noun go together ('the train') might be highlighted by means of colour of print, while the suffixes which indicate part of speech e.g. '-ly', '-ing', could be slightly longer in size or different in slope. The point is that one is trying to get the child to use skills which are potentially available, but which need to be actualized. One is not teaching grammar, but using grammatical skills as a tool.

At the *phonological* level, existing skills can be realized again by using the visual cues of the written sentence. Perhaps the letters in those letter strings representing the most pronounceable and habitual combinations of sounds might be placed closer together than the letters in the rest of the word.

The outstanding feature of language skill as a whole is its *productivity* (see p. 22). Items can be combined in a multitude of different ways, and the language behaviour of children who are learning to read will be productive in this way. Why not, then, use this productive skill as an additional cue? The teacher may employ the non-linguistic environment for this purpose. Punch may hit Judy, manipulated by the child, and the teacher may arrange the written words in front of the stage. The child may then make Judy hit Punch, and the teacher may reverse the order of the words. Later, children may manipulate puppets and words, and later still the words on their own. Manipulation of different language items could be achieved by the child. He could use a series of graded items, which could be fitted together like Leggo. The earliest items might be large-scale units like subject phrase 'The long train', verb phrase 'is steaming', adverbial phrase 'through the tunnel'. There are only two possible orders of these units. However, division into word units allows many more combinations. So does an increase in the number of different larger scale units. The purpose is to employ the productive capacity of the child to help him learn the new spatial skill; using the same letter strings in many different but correct positions increases the likelihood of their recognition and association with combinations of speech sounds.

The use of all possible available skills to make the acquisition of the new sub-skill easier implies that these other skills are in fact available. In other words, it is assumed that children must have attained *a certain level of language development* before the learning of reading can begin. To have attained such a level is not only necessary for acquiring the visuo-spatial skills and for associating letter strings with speech sounds; it is also necessary if the basic purpose of reading is to be achieved: communication.

5 LANGUAGE AND WRITING

Writing is also a means of *communication*; it can in addition be an externalization, an *expression*, of what has been internalized. In both cases it has specific functions. It is not writing in abstract, but writing for a purpose. How often, however, one hears the instruction 'Write about your holidays' or 'Write an essay on humour'. Write about your holidays to whom? For what purpose? Why write an essay, which is an uncommon literary form?

First, consider some of the possible *communicative* functions of writing. One can leave written instructions about how to work a piece of machinery; apply for a job; complain about a piece of shoddy workmanship; tell a friend what one has been doing; draw up an agenda for a meeting; write a report for a meeting's consideration: write labels describing objects at an exhibition or in a classroom.

In each case the communicative purpose is evident; others have to understand what you have written. And the skills they use to do so are *linguistic* in nature. The first requirement of successful writing, then, is that it should be understood, by means of the reader's language skills. Of course, there are less cues available than for oral communication. One cannot point, raise one's voice, pause, or raise one's eyebrows in print. As a result, writing has to provide more specifically linguistic clues. Sentences have to be finished and words written that would have been left unuttered. Writing to communicate will therefore be particularly difficult for working-class boys, whose spoken English is fragmented and who leave many things unsaid because they share so many implicit assumptions.

Communication will also only be achieved effectively if the right *register* of language is employed (see p. 78). There are certain styles and vocabularies appropriate for love letters which are not suitable for (most) job applications. They are not suitable because job applications are a form of communication, and communication is a social situation. The social relationship of a prospective employer to an employee is different from that of lovers to each other. In fact, different roles are being played, and as we saw in Chapter 8, different language registers are used in different roles. The implication is then, that writing in the classroom should be for a specific purpose.

Writing is not only a means of communication; it is also a means of *expression*. Expression is the externalization of internalized language; making potentially public what is essentially private. Internalized language can be connected with the self-concept, with attitudes, or with more intellectual operations. The expression of internalized language means that a pupil must formulate into words feelings or attitudes which he may not have expressed even to himself before. Such expression in writing is thus a very private performance. It is writing for himself; for he may reveal to himself aspects of his personality of which he was not previously fully aware. The potential of this sort of writing for making pupils aware of their self-concept is thus clear. Its irrelevance to communication is also clear, since there is no reader to whom it is addressed. There is, therefore, no need of grammatical completion, nor of the use of an appropriate register; for since this is a private and not a social occasion, there are no roles being played, and therefore no registers to observe.

The teacher has to be very skilful in eliciting this sort of writing, and very sensitive in reading it (if he does so at all). One can understand why so few of us are willing to shrug off our academic and instructional role to make the effort. Most of the writing in the classroom does not fulfil either a communicative or an expressive function. It is, in fact, *reproduction* of what the pupil has read and heard. Its function is to provide feedback to the teacher and marks for his mark-book. The feedback function is worth while, though one may ask why the pupil needs to write down his answers. Practice for examinations? Of course, feedback as to whether the pupil has understood is only possible if the reproduction is in the writer's own words; if, that is, he gives the teacher back the essential content of the teacher's explanation rather than copies it verbatim. The reproductive use of writing, then, has a limited feedback function, but this does not justify its present dominance in classroom practice.

6 SUMMARY

The two basic functions of language, communication and the regulation of behaviour, should be reflected in the nature of the language behaviour used in the classroom. Communication should be two-way, giving pupils practice in producing language behaviour as well as in understanding it. The internalized language used in regulating one's behaviour should be expressed, whether the internalized language is used for intellectual, personal, or social functions. Reading and writing were treated as particular language skills, and the same recommendations were made in their case as in the case of spoken language, since they, too, serve the processes of communication and expression.

10 *Psychological Background*

I PSYCHOLOGICAL THEORY

Students may be relieved and colleagues will certainly be astonished that the name of not a single psychologist has been quoted in the first nine chapters. There are several reasons for this. Firstly, text is very much more difficult to follow if it is interspersed with such items as Smith (1965), let alone Miller, Galanter, and Pribram (1960)! Secondly, if one quotes psychologists, one has to try to do justice to their particular views. Then one has to weigh up the merits of different views, and come to a conclusion. Usually, a clear decision is impossible; if it were, there would not be disagreement. The student is often left with the feeling that since nobody knows, he might as well stick to his own common sense.

I have, therefore, put forward my own views. These have often gone beyond the available experimental evidence. However, I feel that they do represent the feelings of a large number of colleagues. I have indicated those areas in which there is most disagreement, for example, the extent of the innate contribution to language acquisition and the part language plays in thinking. Still, I may have distorted the evidence and misinterpreted current trends as a result of my own preconceptions. For those who suspect that this is true, I am providing a brief overview of the field and some references, so that they can go to the evidence for themselves.

Psychologists study human beings (or at least most of them do). As a result, they bring their own assumptions about the nature of human beings to their work. They choose to do those sorts of experiments which most reinforce their assumptions. One sort of psychologist stresses the importance of *experience*. He supposes that nurture rather than nature, environment rather than heredity, is the origin of human behaviour. As a result, he carries out experiments which give

H

people certain experiences, and then observes the difference in their behaviour. He can, for example, teach pigeons to play ping-pong, or rats to maintain a certain work-rate when they press a bar in their cage. He can devise teaching programmes which result in the learner being able to do things he could not do before.

An alternative type of psychologist stresses the importance of the *person* himself rather than the experience he undergoes. In the case of children, he stresses the fact that there are biologically determined stages of development. These limit what the child can acquire from experience. However, once the right stage of development has been reached, little experience is required for the child to acquire the skills appropriate to the stage. This type of psychologist chooses different types of tasks which require, according to him, different sorts of thinking. Then he notes that children of a certain age succeed, whereas those slightly younger fail at one type of task; but both groups succeed at a different type of task. He therefore concludes that the first type demanded a mode of thinking and therefore a level of development higher than the second type.

Of course, it is almost impossible to distinguish the effects of heredity and environment. Work with identical twins shows both how much more alike they are than less close relatives; and yet, how much they differ when put into different environments. By way of reaction to both the extreme positions caricatured above, many psychologists have come to talk about human beings as if they were *computers*; that is, we are considered as information-processing machines. In a computer, what you feed in is important; so is what you get out of the machine, since it often acts as feedback input; but what is inside the machine is also important, since it acts upon what you put in, and produces what you get out. So this analogy dehumanizes us, but at least it stresses that experience, behaviour, and the brain are involved. But a computer cannot change its hardware or its software in the way that children change as a result of the interaction of input and natural maturation.

You will have spotted these three approaches in different

places in the first nine chapters. The importance of *experience* is implied in the possibility of language remediation, for example, and in the recommended careful programming of learning. The importance of *maturation* is particularly clear in Chapter 6, where the stages of cognitive growth are taken to limit the effect language has on thinking. And the effect of thinking about *information-processing* is clear in the discussion of language as skill (Chapter 3); for there the effects of input, output, and the structure the person imposes on them, are all stressed. The writer has in brief been eclectic; he has picked out what he feels to be best in different approaches.

2 SOME FURTHER READING

The reader might first like to satisfy himself that the overall view of the part played by language in education is shared by other psychologists. A far more experienced writer has written a book similar in some ways to this in aim, scope and readership (Lewis, 1969).

Turning to the chapters in turn, the way in which human beings interact in a communication situation (Chapter 1) is attractively described by Argyle (1967). He pays particular attention to all the non-linguistic cues involved.

A general text which describes the approach of educational psychology (see Chapter 2), and which gives a systematic overview of its findings is that of Stones (1966). This book does not presuppose any prior psychological knowledge. An alternative is Lovell (1957, but be sure to get the most recent edition).

Coming to more detailed psychological work, the psychological processes involved in language behaviour (Chapter 3) are described by Carroll (1964). This book is written for beginning psychology students and presupposes a slight knowledge of psychology. It is by now to some extent out of date. A more detailed and up-to-date survey is the writer's (Herriot, 1970) but this is theoretical in emphasis and presupposes considerable psychological background. The most complete book of readings is that of Jakobovitz and Miron

(1967), and a cheaper volume is that of Oldfield and Marshall (1968); books of readings are reprints of key chapters in books or articles in scientific journals. The best introduction for anyone interested in linguistics rather than psychology is Lyons (1968).

The development of language (Chapter 4) is considered by Brown (1965) in two brilliant chapters. There are also articles on language development in the books of readings quoted above.

Language deficit (Chapter 5) of the cultural variety is dealt with at length by Lawton (1968), who gives a full account of the work of Bernstein. Teachers might find the book by Molloy (1965) useful for its practical hints on remediation. Mittler's (1970) comprehensive volume contains detailed information on language deficits and many other mental and physical handicaps.

The connections of language and thinking (Chapter 6) are covered in many different books. The student should first familiarize himself with a simple introduction to the work of Piaget (Beard, 1969). Flavell (1963) gives a far more detailed and complex account. Other more advanced books on the development of thinking are Hunt (1961) and Lunzer and Morris (1968). The writer's Chapter 6 includes some of the ideas of Bruner, expressed in some detail in Chapters 1 and 2 of Bruner, Olver and Greenfield (1966).

Chapters 7 and 8 concern the personal and social development of the child. Very little introductory material is available in these areas. Physical growth is described by Tanner (1961) but personal and social development are only dealt with in a manner suitable for beginning psychology students, rather than related to teaching: the Prentice-Hall Foundations of Modern Psychology Series offers Mussen (1963), Lazarus (1965), and Murray (1964). Mussen, Conger and Kagan (1963) give a fuller account, but still within the grasp of students. Goffman (1956) gives a brilliant account of social behaviour as playing a part, and Hoyle (1969) provides a basic book for students on the nature of the teacher's role in particular; Fleming (1959) may also prove useful. Very good material is available in the

Connexions series, published by Penguin Education, for eliciting and illuminating pupils' attitudes on current questions.

Language in the classroom is interestingly described in the recent report by Barnes (1969). Ways of teaching language behaviour are outlined by Flower (1966), and a good introduction to the teaching of reading is that of Roberts (1969).

Bibliography

ARGYLE, M. (1967), *The Psychology of Interpersonal Behaviour*. Penguin Books.

BARNES, D. (1969), *Language, the Learner, and the School*. Penguin Books.

BEARD, R. M. (1969), *An Outline of Piaget's Developmental Psychology* (The Student's Library of Education). Routledge and Kegan Paul.

BROWN, R.W. (1965), *Social Psychology*. The Free Press.

BRUNER, J. S., OLVER, R. R., and GREENFIELD, P. M. (1966), *Studies in Cognitive Growth*. Wiley.

CARROLL, J.B. (1964), *Language and Thought*. Prentice-Hall.

FLAVELL, J. (1963), *The Developmental Psychology of Jean Piaget*. Van Nostrand.

FLEMING, C. M. (1959), *The Social Psychology of Education* (second edition). Routledge and Kegan Paul.

FLOWER, F. D. (1966), *Language and Education*. Longmans.

GOFFMAN, E. (1956), *The Presentation of Self in Everyday Life*. Edinburgh University Press.

HERRIOT, P. (1970), *An Introduction to the Psychology of Language*. Methuen.

HOYLE, E. (1969), *The Role of the Teacher* (The Student's Library of Education). Routledge and Kegan Paul.

HUNT, J. MC. V. (1961), *Intelligence and Experience*. The Ronald Press.

JAKOBOVITZ, L. A., and MIRON, M. S. (eds.) (1967), *Readings in the Psychology of Language*. Prentice-Hall.

LAWTON, D. (1968), *Social Class, Language and Education*. Routledge and Kegan Paul.

LAZARUS, R. S. (1965), *Personality and Adjustment*. Prentice-Hall.

LEWIS, M. M. (1969), *Language and the Child*. National Foundation for Educational Research.

LOVELL, K. (1957), *Educational Psychology and Children*. University of London Press.

LUNZER, E. A., and MORRIS, J. F. (eds.) (1968), *Development in Human Learning*. Staples.

LYONS, J. (1968), *Introduction to Theoretical Linguistics*. Cambridge University Press.

MITTLER, P. (ed.) (1970), *The Psychological Assessment of Mental and Physical Handicaps*. Methuen.

MOLLOY, J. S. (1965), *Teaching the Retarded Child to Talk*. University of London Press.

MURRAY, E. J. (1964), *Motivation and Emotion*. Prentice-Hall.

MUSSEN, P. H. (1963), *The Psychological Development of the Child*. Prentice-Hall.

MUSSEN, P. H., CONGER, J. J., and KAGAN, J. (1957), *Child Development and Personality*. Harper and Row.

OLDFIELD, R. C., and MARSHALL, J. C. (eds.) (1968), *Language*. Penguin Books.

ROBERTS, G. (1969), *Reading in Primary Schools* (The Student's Library of Education). Routledge and Kegan Paul.

STONES, E. (1966), *An Introduction to Educational Psychology*. Methuen.

TANNER, J. M. (1961), *Education and Physical Growth*. University of London Press.

Glossary and Index

Glossary

This defines terms as they are used in this book.

accommodation
The changing of schemata to accord with new experience.

assimilation
The structuring of experience to accord with existing schemata.

autonomy
The independence of the self-concept from its origins.

codes of language
Different levels of language behaviour employed by different socio-economic classes.

communication
The process of sending and receiving messages.

concrete operations
The earlier sub-stage of operational thinking, in which symbols cannot yet be employed in a closed system.

conservation
The understanding that a principle holds invariant regardless of the specific circumstances.

cues
Signals that certain behaviour is appropriate.

distinctive features
Those features of all known speech sounds which distinguish them from each other.

expansion
The process by which a mother replies in a fuller, more grammatical way, to her child's utterance.

expression
The use of language behaviour in cases where it is usually suppressed.

feedback
The information from the results of previous behaviour which can be used to modify subsequent behaviour.

formal operations	The later sub-stage of operational thinking, in which a closed system of symbols is employed.
form class	The grammatical function of a word in a sentence.
grammatical skill	The skill of applying abstract principles to combine morphemes into sentences.
identification	The use of another person as a model.
inflexions	Morphemes which are not words but which signal the grammatical functions of words.
internalization	The process which results in the possibility of activating structures in the brain without producing the behaviour which they regulate.
language	The processes in the brain which regulate speech.
morpheme	The smallest units of language behaviour which have a grammatical function.
operational thinking	The stage of development of thinking at which one can use symbols to represent experience and combine and manipulate them according to rules.
peer group	A group of people of roughly the same age or status (especially adolescents).
phoneme	A set of speech sounds which, although different, are perceived to be the same by the listener. The basic sound unit of a language, from combinations of which all morphemes are composed.
phonological skill	The skill of perceiving and producing the sounds of speech.

productivity	A property of language behaviour: the possibility of combining units of speech in many different ways.
redundancy	The existence of more items in a message than would be necessary for its reception in perfect conditions.
registers of language	Areas of language behaviour suitable for use in certain communication situations only.
regulation	The direction of behaviour by the brain.
reproduction	The pupil's presentation back to the teacher of the basic content of what he has been taught.
reversibility	The possibility of performing (in reverse) an operation with symbols.
role	The part played by a person in a social situation.
schema (plural — *schemata*)	Structures in the brain which regulate behaviour.
self-concept	The person's idea of who and what sort of person he is.
semantic skill	The ability to select appropriate words singly and in combination.
suggestion	The changing of attitudes by indirect and irrational means.
thinking	The processes in the brain which regulate complex non-linguistic behaviour.

Index

accommodation, 8–9, 32, 63–64, 73
acquisition of language, 30–40
adolescence, 64–66, 70–72
anticipation, 18–19
articulation, 27, 50
assimilation, 8–9, 32, 63–64, 73
attention, 59
attitudes, 66–69, 71–72
automation, 18–19
autonomy, 66

body image, 65
brain, 28–29, 37–38

codes of language, 41–44
communication, 1–9, 38, 43–44, 82–83, 92
comprehension, 45–48
concrete operations, 57–59
conservation, 15, 56

deficits of language, 41–51
definition of roles, 74–75
development
   of attitudes, 66–68, 71–72
   of morality, 66–68, 71–72
   of self-concept, 63–64, 68–72
   of thinking, 7, 15–17, 52–61
   of social roles, 73–81
developmental speech disorders, 50–51
distinctive features, 21, 31
dysphasia, 51

environmental
   context, 8, 26–27, 45–50, 90
   deprivation, 41–44
expansion, 34
experimental control, 11–12
expression, 86

feedback, 2, 18–20, 60, 73
formal operations, 57–59

grammatical skill, 22–23, 32–34, 42, 91

identification, 63
inflexions, 22, 33–34
innate, 37–38
internalization, 53–55, 63, 73, 84–86

learning to read, 88–92
linguistic skill, 27–29
look-and-say, 89–90

maintenance of roles, 75, 78
meaning, 13–14
morphemes, 22

operational thinking, 55–59

peer group, 66, 76
perception, 27–28
perceptual constant, 21
personal development, 62–72
phonic methods, 89
phonological skill, 20–22, 30–32
planning, 19, 23
play, 74, 77
production, 27–29, 45–48
productivity, 22, 30, 57–58, 91–92
psychology, nature of, 10–13
psychological theory, 95–97

reading, 86–92
redundancy, 3–4, 28
reference, 13–14, 35
registers of language, 78, 93
regulation of behaviour, 28–29, 38, 52–54, 84–86
remediation, 44–50

reproduction, 94
reversibility, 56
role, 62, 73–81, 85

schemata, 29, 38
self-concept
  in adolescence, 64–66
  nature of, 62–64, 85
semantic skill, 24–26, 34–37, 90–91
skill, nature of, 7, 18–20
skilled reading, 86–88
social
  context, 7, 49–50
  development, 73–81
spatial skills, 88–89
specific deficit, 50–51
strategies of remediation, 44–46

suggestion, 68
switching of roles, 74, 77–78
symbols, 56–58
systematisation
  of attitudes, 66–68, 71–72
  of the self-concept, 64–66, 70–71

tactics of remediation, 46–50
teaching
  as communication, 5–9
  of language, 44–50
  of reading, 88–92
thinking, 13–17, 52–61

understanding, 3, 5–9, 26–27

writing, 92–94